Welcome

The iPad mini, without a doubt, is the best iPad to date. What looked at first to be a knee-jerk reaction to an ever-expanding line-up of rivals could yet turn out to be Apple's trump card.

It's close to the size of a paperback, so perfect for reading digital books on the go. Its resolution is the same as the iPad 2, yet the smaller screen means the pixels are closer together, so it comes close to rivalling the Retina Display in the more expensive, high-end iPad. Despite this, it's still large enough to display interactive magazines, and it has access to the most popular mobile gaming platform yet developed. It runs an unrivalled range of tablet apps, and with both wifi-only and cell-enabled editions it makes it easy to get online wherever you happen to be.

If you haven't already worked it out for yourself, the iPad mini has bowled us over.

You can't really appreciate just how cute, useable and easy it is to carry until you get your hands

on one, but once you do you'll see that it makes the full-sized iPad, thin though it may be, feel somehow oversized. Its rivals, meanwhile, many of which lack the finesse of the mini's glass and metal case, pencil-thin body and natty Smart Cover, lack its general finesse.

Whether you're tempted to splash out on an iPad mini, having a tough time choosing between that and a full-sized iPad 2 or iPad with Retina Display, or you've just jumped on the iPad mini bandwagon, this is the book for you. We'll walk

you through the various options, show you how to get set up and, once you're at home with the native applications, how to install your own choice of third-party downloads.

We'll show you how to set up a free account with Apple's iCloud service so you can track a lost iPad mini and share your documents, photos and other data with other iOS devices, your Mac or PC. That way you'll not run the risk of losing anything should misplace it. And... if you do happen to be separated, we'll show you how to locate it online, plotting its exact position on a map so that you can retrieve it.

If you're still not convinced, we can help there, too. The iPad mini is more than just a desirable gadget. It really is one of the most flexible and user-friendly tablet computers around. It looks great, and it works like a dream as it's stable, secure, and easy to use. Read on, and you'll fully appreciate the revolutionary world of truly mobile computing.

Nik Rawlinson

Start here...

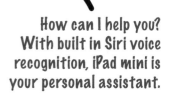

How can I help you? With built in Siri voice recognition, iPad mini is your personal assistant.

iPad mini and iOS 6 make it easy to post to Facebook and Twitter

Swipe to continue...

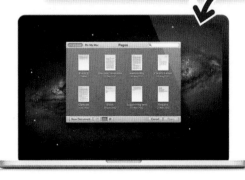

The Independent Guide to the

iPad mini

WRITTEN BY Nik Rawlinson

MANAGEMENT
MagBook Publisher Dharmesh Mistry
Digital Production Manager Nicky Baker
Operations Director Robin Ryan
Managing Director of Advertising Julian Lloyd-Evans
Newstrade Director David Barker
Commercial & Retail Director Martin Belson
Chief Operating Officer Brett Reynolds
Group Finance Director Ian Leggett
Chief Executive James Tye
Chairman Felix Dennis

MAG**BOOK**

LICENSING & SYNDICATION
To license this product, please contact Carlotta Serantoni on +44 (0) 20 7907 6550 or email carlotta_serantoni@dennis.co.uk. To syndicate content from this product please contact Anj Dosaj Halai on +44 (0) 20 7907 6132 or email anj_dosaj-halai@dennis.co.uk.

Chapter 1
Buying an iPad mini

Introducing... iPad mini
The smallest, cutest, best iPad to date

When Apple co-founder Steve Jobs returned after several years spent running another company, he quickly identified Apple's biggest problem. The company wasn't making a profit, because its range of products was simply too large.

It had computers for just about every kind of user: education machines, low-end, high-end and even third-party products that used versions of the operating system that Apple had licensed to them. It was, in effect, competing against itself.

This meant not only that making a decision about what to buy was more difficult for the end-user, but also that Apple was committed to making such a wide variety of products and, somehow, storing them so that they were ready to be shipped to the customer when ordered.

Jobs slashed Apple's range, and maintained just two entry-level and two high end products. Apple has followed this philosophy ever since. In most cases there are no more than three standard options for any product, and in that respect the range of products as a whole is very narrow.

Take its notebooks as a case in point. It only has two lines here: the MacBook Air and the MacBook Pro. Likewise, it has only three desktop products: the iMac, the Mac mini and the Mac Pro. It has just one phone, although three generations remain on sale, and until recently it also had only one size of iPad.

All of that changed in October 2012 when Apple introduced the iPad mini. This wasn't a great surprise, as pundits had been predicting that Apple would make such a move for several months. Other products like the Nexus 7 and Amazon's Kindle Fire HD were both eating into Apple's potential audience by appealing to those who wanted a smaller product. If Apple was to compete then it, too, would have to develop a smaller tablet with which to fight back.

What did surprise most Apple watchers was the price. Amazon's Kindle HD cost less than $200 in the US, but the iPad mini started at $329.

If the iPad mini was the same as all the other tablets on the market then this kind of pricing would have been a disaster. Nobody would pay an extra $129 for more or less the same product. But the iPad mini was quite different, not only in how it worked, but also how it looked.

With just a small number of variations to choose from, it's easy to pick the best iPad mini for your needs.

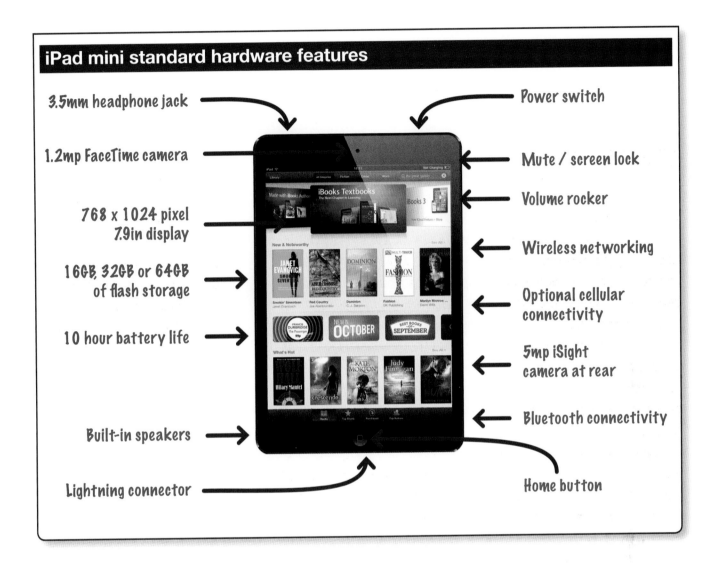

iPad mini standard hardware features

- 3.5mm headphone jack
- 1.2mp FaceTime camera
- 768 x 1024 pixel 7.9in display
- 16GB, 32GB or 64GB of flash storage
- 10 hour battery life
- Built-in speakers
- Lightning connector

- Power switch
- Mute / screen lock
- Volume rocker
- Wireless networking
- Optional cellular connectivity
- 5mp iSight camera at rear
- Bluetooth connectivity
- Home button

It's slim, more attractive, and made of metal and glass. It hooks in to the iOS App Store, which offers an enormous range of third-party software, just like the Amazon Appstore. However, Apple claims that more of these applications have been written specifically for the iPad rather than simply being scaled up phone apps, and because the iPad mini has the same screen resolution as the iPad 2 the vast majority of them will run on the new device without any problem.

That's a boon for anyone who already has an iPad or iPhone as they won't need to buy all of their applications again from scratch. That should save a lot of money and help offset some of the cost of the iPad mini.

Moreover, because it's running the same applications as any other iOS devices you might own it can also access the same content, so any tracks you bought from the iTunes Store on a Mac or PC can be played just as easily on the new iPad mini as they can on an iPhone, iPod or regular iPad. Likewise, movies, TV shows and books transfer smoothly from one to the other.

In much the same way that Apple minimises the range of

Supported languages

iOS 6 English (U.S.), English (UK), Chinese (Simplified), Chinese (Traditional), French, German, Italian, Japanese, Korean, Spanish, Arabic, Catalan, Croatian, Czech, Danish, Dutch, Finnish, Greek, Hebrew, Hungarian, Indonesian, Malay, Norwegian, Polish, Portuguese, Portuguese (Brazil), Romanian, Russian, Slovak, Swedish, Thai, Turkish, Ukrainian, Vietnamese

Keyboards English (U.S.), English (Australian), English (Canadian), English (UK), Chinese - Simplified (Handwriting, Pinyin, Stroke), Chinese - Traditional (Handwriting, Pinyin, Zhuyin, Cangjie, Stroke), French, French (Canadian), French (Switzerland), German (Germany), German (Switzerland), Italian, Japanese (Romaji, Kana), Korean, Spanish, Arabic, Bulgarian, Catalan, Cherokee, Croatian, Czech, Danish, Dutch, Emoji, Estonian, Finnish, Flemish, Greek, Hawaiian, Hebrew, Hindi, Hungarian, Icelandic, Indonesian, Latvian, Lithuanian, Macedonian, Malay, Norwegian, Polish, Portuguese (Portugal), Portuguese (Brazil), Romanian, Russian, Serbian (Cyrillic/Latin), Slovak, Swedish, Thai, Tibetan, Turkish, Ukrainian, Vietnamese

Siri English (U.S., UK, Canada, Australia), Spanish (U.S., Mexico, Spain), French (France, Canada, Switzerland), German (Germany, Switzerland), Italian (Italy, Switzerland), Japanese, Korean, Mandarin (Mainland China, Taiwan), Cantonese (Hong Kong)

Source: Apple iPad mini specs

confusing options within each product line, it has simplified the choices you need to make when buying an iPad mini.

Online options

The fundamental difference between the two halves of the iPad mini product line concerns the way in which each one communicates with the outside world. The cheapest option is to buy a product that can only connect to a wireless network. For the greatest possible flexibility, though, you can also choose an iPad mini that connects to the mobile phone network.

This option has a Nano Sim just like an iPhone 5, but unlike the iPhone it's unable to make voice calls, and it can't send text messages using SMS or MMS (however, it can use Apple's own Messages app to send snort notes – as well as files and photos – to other Messages users on an iOS or OS X device).

Size isn't everything

Once you've decided on your connectivity options you need to settle on a capacity. Each version of the iPad mini comes in a choice of three capacities: 16GB, 32GB or 64GB.

It's easy to imagine that the 64GB option is immediately the best choice, and to a degree, that's true, as it means you can store more on your device at any one time. However, it also significantly increases the up-front cost, and if you are willing to take only a subset of your content around with you at any one time you can make a significant saving by buying

Native apps

App Store	Messages
Calendar	Music
Camera	Newsstand
Clock	Notes
Contacts	Photo Booth
FaceTime	Photos
iTunes	Reminders
Game Centre	Safari
Mail	Videos
Maps	

a lower capacity device and synchronising it with your Mac or PC on a regular basis.

This makes a lot of sense. After all, there's only so much music you can listen to at any one time, a limit to the number of videos you can watch, and a finite number of books you can read. In this respect, buying a lower capacity device is unlikely to limit your media consumption choices. Once you've grown tired of an album, simply remove it from your iPad mini and it will still be available in your main iTunes library on your Mac or PC to be restored to the iPad mini when you want to listen to it again. Likewise, when you've finished reading a magazine, remove it from the device to save space so that you can download another, and if you want to reread it you can simply retrieve it from the publisher's online archive.

Choosing which iPad mini is right for you isn't therefore a simple case of opting for the highest capacity you can afford. Instead, think about how you will use the device at how often

you'll be able to synchronise it with your computer. When you've worked that out, buy the product that best suits your lifestyle.

iCloud helps out...

Even if you travel often and don't get a chance to frequently synchronise your iPad with your home or office computer, you still needn't necessarily opt by default for the 64GB product. Apple's free online iCloud service keeps a record of your all purchases made on your Apple ID. So, as long as you can access either the cellphone network or a Wi-Fi hub, you can download a new copy of any track, video, TV show or book wherever you are when ever you want to consume it.

iCloud can also be used to sync documents created using many third-party apps so that they are safely backed-up centrally and easily retrieved at a later date.

The best tactic when choosing a capacity for your new iPad mini, therefore, is to look first at the 32GB product that sits in the

middle of the lineup and decide whether you can downgrade and save some money, or need to upgrade and spend a little more to meet your own particular requirements.

Standard issue

All iPad minis have a 7.9 inch display, with a native resolution of 768 x 1024 pixels. This is the same as the iPad 2 resolution. By squeezing the same number of pixels into a physically smaller panel, Apple has reduced the size of each one, and so the level of grain in the image is greatly reduced and the resulting display is more pleasant to look at.

All iPad minis feature a dual core Apple A5 processor and a five megapixel camera to the

rear. The sensor is backside illuminated, which means that the electronics that carry the data from the sensor to the processor have been moved to the back so that it can gather more light and render a more accurate image.

There's a second camera at the front for video conferencing, with a native resolution of 1.2 megapixels.

You can connect the iPad mini to your computer using the bundled Lightning Connector, as used on the 4th Gen iPad and iPhone 5. It's smaller than the old 30-pin connector and can be inserted in either orientation, so should cause fewer complications. It's not directly compatible with existing

accessories that were built for 30-pin, but Apple sells an optional adapter.

You can also buy a range of other accessories from Apple, including a shrunken Smart Cover, like the ones for the regular iPad, which attaches itself magnetically to the side of the iPad mini, and automatically sends it to sleep when closed. Lifting it wakes it up again.

Apple's existing Bluetooth keyboard – as well as Bluetooth keyboards from third-party manufacturers – can be used in place of the on-screen keyboard for periods of extended typing. In such an instance, the Smart Cover is again handy as it allows you to prop up the iPad mini

so that the screen more closely resembles that of a regular notebook device.

Although it's smaller, Apple has still managed to include sufficient battery capacity that the iPad mini will run for the same 10 hours is the fourth generation iPad when browsing the web on Wi-Fi, watching video or listening to music. If you're browsing the web on a cellphone network, which drains more power, the battery life is slightly reduced to a still respectable nine hours.

It has built-in speakers and a headphone jack, and can stream content both to AirPort Express for playing back through remote speakers and to Apple TV for displaying on a connected high-definition television.

Unlike the iPad 2 with which it shares many features, the iPad mini can also access Apple's Siri personal assistant. This has been localised for 14 different countries, but performance varies between them, with users in the United States enjoying the widest possible range of features and relevant information.

Model	Wi-Fi only	Wi-Fi and cellular
Capacity	16GB / 32GB / 64GB	
Processor	Apple A5	
Connectivity options	Wireless Ethernet Bluetooth	Wireless Ethernet Bluetooth GSM / EDGE /UMTS / HSPA+ / LTE – or – CDMA / GSM / EDGE / UMTS / HSPA+ / LTE
Display	7.9in encompassing 768 x 1024 pixels	
Front camera	1.2 megapixels	
Rear camera	5 megapixels	
Power	10 hours wireless productivity on Wi-Fi, or 9 hours on cellular data for cellular-enabled model	
Ports and connections	Lightning connector and 3.5mm stereo headphone jack	
Sensors	Digital compass Gyroscope Accelerometer Ambient light sensor	
System requirements	Internet access, OS X 10.6.8 or later, or Windows XP or later	
Size	200 x 134.7 x 7.2mm	
Weight	308g	312g
Colours	Black and Slate, or White and Silver	

iPad mini, iPad or iPhone...
...which one is right for you?

Since they all run the same operating system and applications, you might be left wondering whether you would be better served by an iPhone or a regular iPad than the diminutive iPad mini.

In many instances the choice if a simple matter of personal preference, but a cold comparison of their various merits nonetheless pays serious dividends and helps you make a more informed decision.

iPhone

Naturally the iPhone is the smallest of the three, so simultaneously benefits from being the easiest to carry while offering the poorest typing experience. The iPhone's on-

With the iPad 2 and fourth generation iPad, iPad mini, iPhone 5, iPhone 4S and iPhone 4, Apple's range of iOS products is now almost as large as its regular computer line-up, giving you a broad choice of compatible devices.

screen keyboard does a great job of correcting your mistakes but it's not really practical when it comes to typing out long documents in an application like Pages. Dictation can help to a degree, but that's not viable when you're trying to work on public transport.

Portability aside, the iPhone's trump card is the fact that it's the only one on which you can make regular phone calls, rather than VoIP (Internet) phone calls, so is the best-equipped for keeping you in touch with friends, family and business associates.

Although the iPad and iPad mini can connect to the cellphone network, they can only use it to send and receive data.

Each device can use FaceTime to communicate using both audio and video over a Wi-Fi network while the iPhone 4S and 5 can also use FaceTime over the cellphone network. The iPhone 4 and 4S are both the same size, and are smaller than the iPhone 5, as you can see in our mock-up, below, of each of the products in the line-up. They therefore offer the greatest portability of all.

iPad

The full-blown iPad comes in two flavours. There's either the most recent release – the fourth-generation device – or the iPad 2, which Apple has kept in the line-up to provide a lower-cost entry point for first-time tablet buyers.

The larger form factor makes reading magazines and digital newspapers a more natural experience on the full-size iPad, and when you compare either of these to the iPad mini you'll see that the text on your pages will be larger at the same zoom level, so for anyone with poor eyesight they may make for a better experience overall.

However, bear in mind that the iPad mini shares many of the same components as you'd find in the iPad 2, including the screen resolution. Both have a panel capable of rendering 768 x 1024 pixels, which is fine on a tablet device of just about any size, but better suited to the smaller device. That's because in the iPad mini the pixels are smaller, and so harder to

Don't forget the iPod touch

While comparing the various iOS options, it's important to remember that the iPod touch also runs iOS 6. The latest release can make use of Apple's Siri personal assistant, and although it lacks the iPhone's telephony features it can run most of the same iOS applications, which makes it a great choice for anyone who wants to access their data on the move but doesn't need a device on which they can talk to their friends. In this respect it bears a lot of similarities to the iPad mini, and could be considered the most convenient iOS 6 device of them all.

see, which means you'll get a better, finer screen image when comparing identical content with that displayed on the iPad 2. The fourth-generation iPad has the best screen of all, with a pixel density that Apple refers to as Retina Display as you can't make out the individual pixels at all at regular reading distances.

Although they both have an Apple A5 processor under the hood, the iPad 2 can't make use of Siri, while the iPad mini can. Siri might still not have as many features outside of the US as it does within the States, but it remains a useful tool, and its

abilities are growing by the day, so if you're buying an iPad today that you want to continue using for the next couple of years, it makes sense to sidestep the second-generation iPad and opt for either the full-size fourth-generation iPad, or iPad mini.

The iPad 2 is now the only device of the three not to feature the new Lightning connector for data transfer, so if you already have a range of accessories for an older iPhone or original iPad that you want to use with your new iPad or iPad mini, then you'll need to also purchase a Lightning to 30-pin adaptor.

The complete iOS family
A choice of six devices

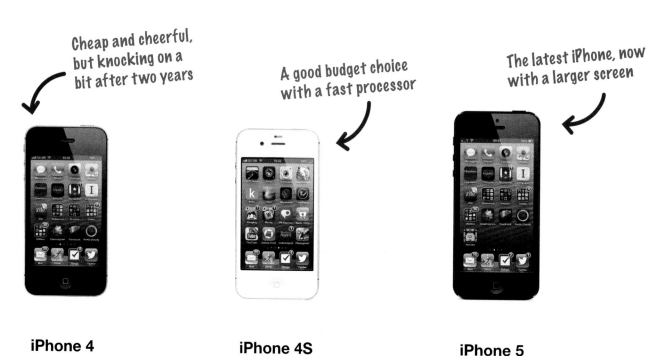

Cheap and cheerful, but knocking on a bit after two years

A good budget choice with a fast processor

The latest iPhone, now with a larger screen

iPhone 4	iPhone 4S	iPhone 5
A4 processor	A5 processor	A6 processor
3.5in display	3.5in display	3.5in display
960 x 640 pixels	960 x 640 pixels	1136 x 640 pixels
8GB memory	16GB memory	16GB / 32GB / 64GB memory
30 pin connector	30 pin connector	Lightning connector
5 megapixel camera	8 megapixel camera	8 megapixel camera
720p video recording	1080p video recording	1080p video recording
300 hours standby	200 hours standby	225 hours standby
10 hours Wi-Fi browsing	9 hours Wi-Fi browsing	10 hours Wi-Fi browsing
–	Siri personal assistant	Siri personal assistant
137 grams	140 grams	112 grams
115.2 x 58.6 x 9.3mm	115.2 x 58.6 x 9.3mm	123.8 x 58.6 x 7.6mm

Like a smaller iPad 2, but with Siri features built-in

Inexpensive entry-level iPad, but missing a few key options

The king of all iPads, it's fast, full-featured and built to last

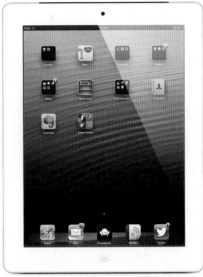

iPad mini	iPad 2	iPad 4th generation
A5 processor	A5 processor	A6X processor
7.9in display	9.7in display	9.7in display
1024 x 768 pixels	1024 x 768 pixels	2048 x 1536 pixels
16GB / 32GB / 64GB memory	16GB memory	16GB / 32GB / 64GB memory
Lightning connector	30 pin connector	Lightning connector
5 megapixel camera	0.6 megapixel camera	5 megapixel camera
1080p video recording	1080p video recording	1080p video recording
— iPad battery standby times not disclosed —		
10 hours Wi-Fi browsing	9 hours Wi-Fi browsing	10 hours Wi-Fi browsing
Siri personal assistant	–	Siri personal assistant
308g (Wi-Fi) / 312g (cellular)	601g (Wi-Fi) / 613g (cellular)	652g (Wi-Fi) / 662g (cellular)
200 x 134.7x 7.2mm	241.2 x 185.7 x 8.8mm	241.2 x 185.7 x 9.4mm

Chapter 2
Using iOS 6

iPad mini and iOS 6
Perfect partners for working and playing on the move

New features iOS 6

Once known as iPhone OS, iOS 6 is Apple's operating system for the iPhone, iPad, iPod touch and Apple TV. It doesn't run the same applications as OS X on the Mac but is built on the same codebase. The name change came about when Apple started to expand the range of platforms on which it could run.

The software that appears on each of these devices is only one half of the equation, though, with the second half being the software development kit (SDK) that Apple makes available to paying developers so that they can write applications for the devices that run it.

To this end, iOS is now one of the best supported operating systems on any platform – not just on tablets – with over half a million applications produced to date. These can be downloaded directly from the iOS App Store application on the iPhone, or through iTunes on a regular Mac or PC. That's quite a turn-around from the early days when Apple announced its first iOS

device – the original iPhone – and declared that the only way anyone would be able to develop their own applications for it would be if they ran through the browser. Without performing that particular about turn, it's highly unlikely you'd be holding an iPad mini today.

While iOS 6 runs on your iPad mini and stores your data locally, it also hooks up to iCloud, Apple's online backup and synchronisation service, which copies iWorks and other documents between your mobile device and a Mac, and automatically transfers photos taken on your iPhone to either iPhoto or Aperture on the Mac, or a dedicated folder on a PC, while at the same time syncing apps, books and media downloads.

You can call up Notification Centre from inside any other app by dragging down on the clock at the top of the iPad mini screen.

The new Maps application in iOS 6 moves away from Google data and initially came in for some criticism upon launch.

It has a built-in Software Update tool that makes it easy to check that you're running the most up-to-date version of the operating system, and a built-in App Store through which you can buy new applications directly without reverting to your Mac or PC. This separately keeps track of any updates to your purchases over time and lets you download free upgrades.

The Notification Centre, which was introduced in iOS 5, centralises all of the messages and alerts spawned by your applications into one easy to find location so you don't have to cancel them all individually. Swipe down from the clock above any app to open it (see grab, left).

iOS 6

iOS 6, as its name suggests, is the sixth iteration of the operating system. It was finally made available to the general public in late summer 2012 after several months of testing among the developer community. It is a free update for users of later iPads but won't work with the original iPad, as it doesn't have the necessary hardware to support it. Such obsolescence is also a good way for Apple to encourage us to upgrade.

How does iOS 6 differ from iOS 5?

If you've used a full-sized iPad in the past, and were just to look at the home screen of an iPad mini running iOS 6, you could be forgiven for thinking that nothing had changed in the move from iOS 5. All of the familiar icons and folders remain in place, Spotlight stays where it always was and your most commonly-used applications can still be organised on a short Dock that appears on each of the Home Screens.

This is misleading, though, as beneath the surface there are many fundamental changes that make the operating system both more robust and more flexible.

The Maps app has had a serious overhaul. Its content was previously provided by Google, but map data is now supplied directly from Apple's own servers, while directions come from the navigation experts at Tom Tom. It has a fresh new look as a result, and keeps the ability to display satellite photography.

The iPad mini shares a first class web browser with the rest of Apple's mobile products in the shape of Safari for iOS.

Apple came in for some criticism when it rolled out its new Maps application, with many users claiming that it didn't maintain the high levels of detail and accuracy that characterised its predecessor. Apple has clearly been working on the issue since then, and Maps is steadily improving as time goes on.

This move away from reliance on Google has also seen Apple drop the YouTube application, which had been a resident on the iPad since the very first release. Prior to that it was shipped on the iPhone and iPod touch where it provided the best means of viewing YouTube videos on any

Apple device. Going forward from the introduction of iOS 6 we'll have to watch YouTube videos through the Safari browser or use a third-party client.

Facebook is now integrated, just like Twitter, and Siri, Apple's voice-recognition assistant, has been upgraded across several territories so that it now knows more about cinema times, sports venues and so on. The inclusion of Siri on the iPad mini is an interesting point, as although it shares the same screen resolution and many of its core components with the iPad 2, that older product can't access the Siri service.

Web browser

The iPad has always been a web access device just as much as it's been a handy gadget for creating your own content, so it's not surprising to discover that it has a first-class web browser built in, in the form of Safari.

You might already know Safari from its desktop and laptop manifestation. It has long been the default browser on the Mac, and is available for Windows, too, despite the fact that it didn't receive a PC update the last time it was revamped on the Mac.

It is fully standards compliant, so you shouldn't have any trouble browsing regular pages, and it makes use of tabs in such a way that, as demonstrated at the iPad mini launch, it leaves the vast majority of your screen free of application clutter to display nice large web pages.

Email client

It's not so long ago that the only practical way to keep up with your email on the move was to

Maps app quick tip

Apple is doing much to improve the performance of its new Maps application, but if you'd rather use the previous Google incarnation, visit *maps.google.com* in the Safari browser and add it as a web application by following the instructions that pop up.

buy a BlackBerry Messenger. This took all of the responsibility for managing your mail our of your hands, delivering it as soon as it was received by the server, and allowing you to reply on the spot.

The iPad does the same courtesy of iCloud, which offers all subscribers a free @me.com addresses. If you prefer not to use iCloud, you can also sign up for push email from third-party providers, or use your own domain.

What does this mean for you? Quite simply, simplicity. Push

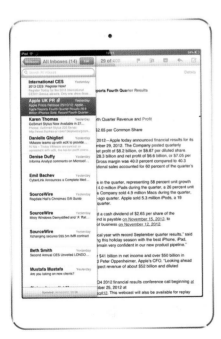

takes all the hassle out of mobile email, because the messages come to you and can be dealt with as soon and as often as you like. Better yet, if you're using iCloud or another IMAP-compatible service, because the email is stored on a remote server you can access it from any device in any location. This means that any email you mark as read on your Mac or PC will also be marked as read on your iPad mini, and any email you send while you're out and about will also appear in the sent items folder on your computer.

As well as iCloud, the iPad mini can connect to a host of other services including Yahoo mail, Gmail and regular Pop3 and IMAP services. For business users, it also works happily with Microsoft Exchange servers, which are common in enterprise set-ups.

It's important to choose the most appropriate server technology for your needs.

While connecting to your own Pop3 server is a simple way to use your regular email address on your iPad mini, you won't be able to synchronise the read and unread status of your messages, or have a record of those messages sent from your iPad mini on your regular computer, unless you cc the same messages back to yourself. IMAP does provide these features and for business users Exchange performs a similar function. Home users should consider hosting their domains on Google's App servers, which let them use the company's Gmail service under their own branding, thus benefiting from the IMAP features.

Maps

Online mapping is nothing new. We've had countless online street maps to choose from since the turn of the millennium. When the first iPhone appeared

The iPad mini's email client lets you connect to a wide range of common server types to keep you productive away from your desk.

The Maps app is smarter than a regular atlas. As well as a normal top-down plan view it can render the scene you're looking at in 3D, with the buildings overlaid using high quality satellite photography.

it used Google's map service for navigation, but with iOS 6 for the iPhone, iPad and now iPad mini, Apple has swapped this out in favour of its own variant.

Despite this, it still boasts many of the features of its predecessor. For example, it allows you to look up local businesses and services – such as car repair shops and pizza restaurants – and ask it to plot the quickest route from your current position to any of the listed results by car, foot or public transport.

The precise means by which your iPad mini can get a fix on your location depends on the model you've bought. If you have a Wi-Fi-only device, it works by referencing your network connection address and using a digital compass to discern your orientation. If you have the Wi-Fi and cellular model, though, it can supplement this with information worked out by triangulating your position on the mobile phone network, and with data received from both the GPS and GLONASS networks (the American and Russian global positioning systems, respectively).

Many applications now make use of positional data of this type to provide location-based dating and games.

Global Positioning System

The global positioning system is a constellation of around two dozen satellites that send a constant stream of location and time data. Suitably-equipped iPad minis compare the data from each satellite and work out how far they are from each one by the errors in the clocks caused by the time it takes for the data to travel through space. Having worked out the difference between each incoming data stream it can accurately work out how far they each are from your current position, and therefore where in the world you are.

Camera

The iPad mini has two built-in cameras; one on the front, just above the screen, and the other around the back.

Of these, the rear camera – known as iSight, like the cameras built into the iMac and Apple's notebook line-up – is the more powerful. It has a resolution of five megapixels, compared to the front FaceTime camera's 1.2 megapixels, and a bright maximum aperture of f/2.4. The lens on each has an infrared coating and the sensor is backside illuminated, which means the circuitry has been moved behind the sensitive surface, which should result in brighter images.

Both cameras can record high definition video, although while this confirms to the 1080p standard on the rear camera it's 720p only at the front. However, this shouldn't be too great an issue, as the front camera's intended use is for video conferencing with the identically-named FaceTime software, which doesn't require a full HD video stream.

The iPad mini allows you to make FaceTime calls over the cellular network, so long as your network provider hasn't put a block on it.

Photos, whichever camera they're recorded by, are automatically geotagged using the built-in location services. These coordinates can be used to position your images on a map in applications like iPhoto and Aperture, or on photo-sharing sites like Flickr.

All of your images are stored in the iPad mini's own Photos application, but if you've signed up for a free iCloud account you can also synchronise the to your other iOS devices, plus a Mac or Windows PC.

Contacts and Calendars

Despite its diminutive size, the iPad mini is a fully-fledged mobile working environment, complete with calendar and address book that you can synchronise with

Sign up for a free iCloud account and you can synchronise your photos across multiple iOS devices plus your Mac or Windows PC.

Synchronisation quick tip

Turn on music, book and app synchronisation through *Settings | iTunes & App Stores* to have the same purchases downloaded to each of your iOS devices and backed up on your Mac or PC. That way, all of your devices will be immediately familiar each time you switch them on, and you'll never lose a purchase again.

your Mac or PC so that wherever you are, and whatever you're doing, you'll know what you need to do next, and who with.

Extra fields in the Contacts app let you tap on an email address to start writing a message, tap an address to see it plotted on a map and tap a URL to open it in Safari.

Music and movie player

The iPad mini features three key media apps. First, **iTunes**, which allows you to download music and videos from the iTunes Store. This media is organised by type in either **Music** (below) or **Videos**. These do just what you'd expect, playing back your purchases and any media you have transferred from your Mac or PC. The Music application understands playlists, allowing you to organise your music or play a shuffled selection.

The videos app plays full-screen in landscape orientation, giving you the best portable environment to catch up on movies that you don't have time to watch at home.

Each of these applications is compatible with Apple's AirPlay system, allowing you to play back your media on a regular television or external speakers using AirPlay hardware, such as Apple TV or AirPort Express. These are separate purchases, but thanks to their seamless integration they enhance the iPad experience.

iBooks

Apple has long been one of the largest retailers of digital music, and with iBooks it's carving out a reputation for itself in digital ebooks, too.

iBooks was updated to version 3 on the same day that the company announced the iPad mini, and it now features new reading modes including a

Although you might use iTunes to play music on your Mac or PC, it's only used for downloads on iPad mini. To play back your tracks here, turn to the Music app instead.

iBooks, and the iBookstore, are helping Apple to sell electronic books in the same way that it does with digital downloads.

seamless scrolling option that does away with turning pages.

Buying books is quick and easy, as the iBookstore uses the same login credentials as the iTunes Store and iCloud.

Mainstream books are generally slightly cheaper than the equivalent printed volumes, and many out-of-copyright books, such as Pride and Prejudice or Emma, are free.

Newsstand lets you subscribe to the electronic versions of your favourite digital magazines, so that you can read them wherever you like, and carry a whole selection at once.

Because iBooks uses the industry standard ePub format you can also download a lot of other books that don't appear in Apple's own store from online book repositories such as Project Gutenberg, and upload them directly to your iPad mini.

Newsstand

iPad mini is the perfect device on which to read magazines, as well as digital books.

Shortly after the launch of the original full-size iPad, many publishers developed their own applications through which iPad owners could subscribe to their publications. Apple has since tidied things up by introducing Newsstand, which gives all of your subscriptions and one-off purchases a place to live without cluttering up the rest of your iPad home screens.

Newsstand (below) simplifies the task of keeping subscriptions up to date, with a central app through which you can organise your incoming magazines and a direct link to the store to buy new issues. New magazines are paid for using your regular Apple App Store credentials and associated payment method.

With social networking tools built in to the very core of iOS 6, it's easy to share your photos and thoughts with your friends on Facebook and your followers on Twitter, however popular you are.

Social networking

Twitter and Facebook are both built in to iOS 6. Twitter had been a part of the iPad since iOS 5, but Facebook integration was always likely sooner or later.

By baking these social networks into the core of its mobile OS, Apple makes it easy to share content, including photos, with your contacts, as Facebook and Twitter appear on the sharing shortcuts built into its pre-installed applications.

The iOS Twitter and Facebook features (above) work hand in hand with the Twitter and Facebook apps, which are free downloads from the App Store.

Reminders

Reminders (below) is a fairly simple tool in which to track a list of jobs that need to be completed. You don't have to tap them out in order, so can pop them in whenever they occur to you. You can then set reminders based on either an arbitrary deadline or a location.

So, if you have to make a phone call at 3pm, you'd enter that with a deadline of 15:00 hrs.

Alternatively, if you knew that you needed to buy apples the next time you're passing by the grocer's shop, but didn't know when that would be, you'd set a reminder based on location. Your iPad mini would then use its built-in GPS receiver, if it had one, or its Wi-Fi and digital compass if it didn't, but was in range of a wireless network to track your location, and when it detected that you were near the grocer's it would pop up a reminder to go in and buy your apples.

Reminders appear on screen in the middle of the display, accompanied by an audible beep

Reminders synchronise across all iOS and OS X devices through iCloud, so long as you're running a recent operating system.

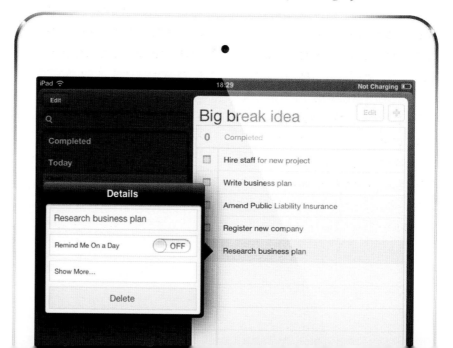

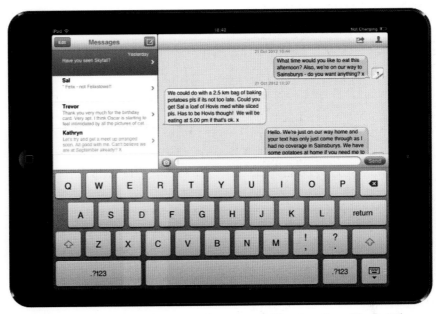

Messages lets you send notes, photos and files to other iPad, iPhone, iPod touch and Mac users for free without using SMS.

(assuming you haven't muted the speaker) and a short vibration. They also synchronise through your iCloud account so that the same notes appear on your iPad mini, iPad, iPhone, iPod touch and Mac, so long as you're running a sufficiently recent edition of the operating system.

Messages

Although the iPad mini doesn't have built-in SMS features like the iPhone, you can still send and receive short messages, along with photos and files, using the built-in Messages application, which also syncs with an app of the same name on the Mac.

Each message is threaded with those that come before and after it to present an easy-to-follow conversation stream, and individual postings even appear in bubbles (see above).

By synchronising across each device, you can leave off a conversation on your iPhone and pick it up again later on when using your iPad, iPhone or Mac, if you have one.

On-screen keyboard

The iPad mini, iPad, iPod touch and iPhone have all done away with physical buttons. Apart from the power button, mute switch, volume control and Home button, there are no external moving parts on the iPad mini, as all of the other buttons have been moved into the software realm and are rendered as graphics on the touchscreen – including the regular keyboard.

This is very intelligent, and while the keys are small (how else would you fit them all onto the screen in portrait mode?), the iPad mini's touch-sensitive membrane is accurate enough

to save you from making many mistakes (beware that reaching across to use it upside down can lead to some missed keystrokes).

Even if you have set your language to English, you can still access a wide variety of international characters using the regular iPad mini keyboard simply by holding down your finger on the character closest to the one you want to pop up international alternatives (see below).

Spotlight
Find anything, anywhere, in an instant

Spotlight is Apple's revolutionary search tool. It first appeared on the Mac as part of OS X and has since been rolled out onto the iPad mini as part of iOS 6.

Spotlight makes it easy for you to find anything on your device, regardless of whether you're searching for data, an application, a contact or a file. Simply typing in related words should be enough to return a positive result.

In the example to the right, we typed in news and it called up a selection of emails and apps. Further up the list it had shown relevant addresses from our Contacts book, while further down we have notes received using Messages, and options to search the web and Wikipedia.

Spotlight as a launcher

In many ways, Spotlight is the ideal file browser. If you can't remember which folder you used to file a particular application then you only need tap its name into the Spotlight search bar and it

will appear in the list, so that all you then need do is tap on it to run it. This alone could save an awful lot of hunting and tapping about various screens.

You'll find Spotlight by swiping all of your Home Screens to the right until you get to the very left-most screen. This will appear as a dimmed overlay on top of your Home Screen background with the regular keyboard at the bottom. There are no other controls in the app itself, so to change anything you'll need to head back to the iPad mini's central settings.

Below: drag all the way right to call up the Spotlight search box

Spotlight evolution

Spotlight first appeared on Apple's desktop and laptop operating system, OS X, and made its way onto its portable devices with the release of iOS 3.0. It has seen several subtle improvements over the years, but on the whole it retains the familiar core functionality. The latest enhancements are quite minor, running simply to a little piece of additional metadata tagged to the end of applications appearing in the search results to indicate which folder they reside within,

---

How to: Change how Spotlight works

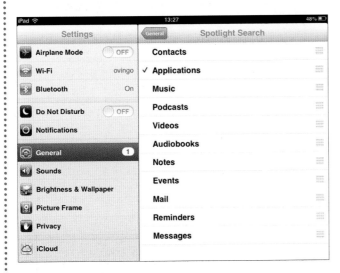 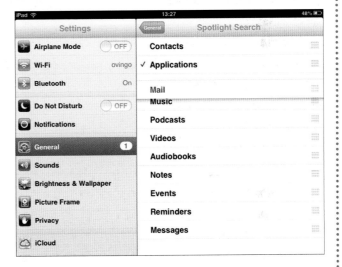

[1] It's important to set up Spotlight to work however is best for you so that you can find your assets with the least hassle possible. Tap Settings | General | Spotlight Search to enter the Spotlight settings pane.

Items with a tick beside them will appear in the Spotlight search results. As you can see, we currently have our iPad mini set to only show us matching Applications in our results. To activate further categories, tap on them. Tap again on any category that already has a tick beside it to remove it from the search results.

[2] Naturally you'll work at your most efficient when the results you need most frequently appear at the top of the Spotlight Search list. You should therefore use the drag handles on the right-hand edge of each category to move it up or down until you have arranged the list in your preferred order.

You can reposition as many categories as you choose in this way, and over time you will probably find that your needs change, so while you might have your Applications at the top of the list to start with, as your inbox becomes more densely populated, Mail could take precedence

Contacts
The simple way to keep track of friends and family

Throughout the development of its mobile operating system, Apple's Contacts application has become more and more important.

In the earliest version of iOS, when it appeared on the original iPhone, there was no Contacts app at all, and to find your friends' details you had first to open the phone application and navigate to your contacts from there using the bottom toolbar.

A few months later, and a few updates down the line, iPhone OS – as it was known back then – finally incorporated a proper address book, and although the app is now called Contacts, rather than Address Book, many of its features and much of its appearance remain unchanged to this day.

Naturally enough, the iPad – and even the iPad mini – afford the application far more space than it can be given on the iPhone, and so the actual contacts book acts in a very similar manner to novels read through iBooks. The contacts themselves are organised using tabbed pages, with a list of your friends, family and so on running down the left-hand page, and the whole of the right hand side given over to a selected contact's details.

Address groups

If you've set up groups in Outlook or, on the Mac, in Address Book or Contacts, these groups will be carried across to Contacts

---

Address synchronisation

Contacts is designed to work in concert with the Contacts or Address Book applications on OS X (they're essentially the same thing, but their names differ depending on which version of OS X you're running) or Outlook on the PC. Each of these applications can be set to synchronise their contents over iCloud.

Check that your iPad mini is drawing down your contacts from the server by tapping Settings | Mail, Contacts, Calendars | iCloud and setting the slider beside contacts to ON.

Tap the tab to switch
to the Groups view
to help organise your
Contacts book

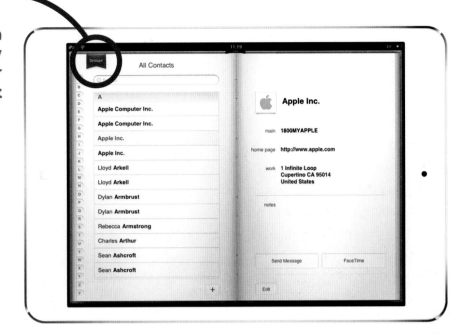

on your iPad mini when you
synchronise over iCloud. You'll
find them by tapping the groups
tab at the top of the left-hand
page, and can selectively turn
on and off the groups you do or
don't want to see in the contacts
book. Note that some groups are
in fact subgroups of others, so in

Contacts and other iOS applications

You might find that you very rarely access your friends' contact details
through the contacts application, and that most of your interaction with
the data will be through other applications. For example, start typing a
name in Mail and it automatically searches the contacts list for matches
and calls up a list of possible options so you only need to tap the
one you want. Likewise, if your contacts' records include their Twitter
names, if you choose Twitter as a method by which to share photos,
map locations, links and so on, it will again auto complete these names
as you start typing them by dropping down a list of possible matches
that's shortened and refined as you carry on typing.

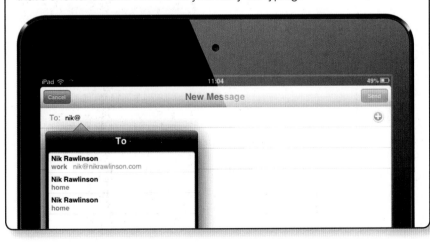

the example over the page, if we
tapped All iCloud, it would hide
each of the groups within it.

Other data is drawn down
from external sources, and again
we can see that over the page
with the Facebook group, which
includes entries added to their
own profiles by our friends on
that social networking site. In
many cases this gives us access
to their phone numbers, screen
names and dates of birth even if
we didn't know them before.

Adding a new contact

Of course, there will be times
when you need to exchange
contact details with somebody
on the spot and it's often easier
to enter those details directly

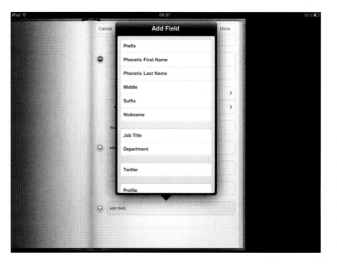

Custom fields let you add supplementary data to your Contacts' individual entries.

into your Contacts book there and then rather than taking their business card home with you and tapping it in later on.

You can easily add contact details directly on your iPad mini by returning to the regular view and tapping the plus at the bottom of the left-hand page. Step through the various boxes in the dialogue that appears, entering the details you know, and optionally add an image by tapping the Add Photo box beside the name. Images can be drawn from your existing photo library or, if the contact is with you, you can take a new photo

using one of the iPad mini's built-in cameras.

You'll notice that while the default contacts view has the most common fields already catered for, such as mobile phone, home and work email addresses, and homepage, there are some obvious omissions, such as job title. You can add these manually by scrolling to the bottom of the input screen and tapping Add Field (see above). This calls up a list of options for you to choose from.

Some of these options might still not deliver quite what you are after at first glance, but many of them hide supplementary options in pop up dialogues. For example, tap Add Field followed by Profile, and by default it will pick Facebook as the profile type.

However, tapping the Facebook header cell pulls up a list of common alternatives such as Twitter, Flickr and LinkedIn or, if you choose, you can add your own custom service by simply entering its name.

Some groups are sub-groups of others, such as the ones listed below iCloud here. Deselecting All iCloud unchecks them all.

Complete Guide to
iPhone
Photography

LEARN HOW TO...

SHOOT LIKE A PRO
EDIT ON YOUR IPHONE
SHARE YOUR PHOTOS

PLUS...

TIPS • TRICKS • ADVICE

Newsstand

Your favourite mags and newspapers... without the paper

Apple has already revolutionised the way we buy and consume music, is well on the way to doing the same with movies and TV, and is looking to emulate Amazon's success in the world of digital books, so it's only natural that it should be showing more than a passing interest in magazines.

The earliest iPad magazines

The iPad is the ideal device on which to consume the next generation of newspapers and mags, as its bright colour screen and extremely thin form factor are both convenient and attractive. The iPad mini makes things even more convenient as it lets us tuck a whole month's-worth of reading in our bags or coat pockets without either the bulk or weight of the printed equivalents.

You don't need to pop by the shop for a paper any more. Newsstand lets you download your favourite publication while you tuck into breakfast.

No wonder publishers were quick to realise that it could be just the solution they needed to declining print-based audiences. They quickly tooled up a new generation of layout artists and designers with all the kit they needed to create iPad-friendly versions of their existing publications and started selling them through the App Store.

This new generation of magazines was an immediate success, simultaneously converting existing print readers to the digital alternative and finding new audiences right around the world, who were

attracted by the lower prices that resulted from not having to ship printed magazines by air and the increased choice they had when they weren't restricted to the limited shelf space of their local newsagent.

The trouble was, if you subscribed to a handful of magazines in the early days, and on top of these downloaded as many free titles as you wanted, your iPad home screen could quickly become a cluttered, jumbled mess of icons, each of which looked just like any other app. Something had to be done.

Newsstand organises your magazines in the same way as it does books in the iBooks app, stacking them on shelves and linking back to an online store

Enter Newsstand

Apple came up with a solution: Newsstand. This appears on all iPads minis, iPad, iPhones and iPod touches running iOS 5 or later, and looks like a small set of shelves on your home screen.

Tap it to expand the shelves to their full size and you'll see that they are a dedicated home for these magazine applications, keeping them separate from your real apps and also allowing you to monitor when new issues are ready to download, as each title's

cover will be overlaid with a blue strap when it's been updated.

Just like regular apps, magazines can only be downloaded through Apple's

dedicated store, accessed from within the Newsstand app by tapping the Store button. This is good news for avid readers as it means you don't have to think about manually updating your collection or hunting around several shops to see who has the latest issue in stock. Better, as all purchases are made using your existing Apple ID all of your payment details are already in place. Keeping up with the news has never been so easy, as we'll show you over the page.

Apple's multiplying content stores

Apple's first content store was the iTunes Music Store, which only sold singles and albums. It's since been renamed as simply the iTunes Store to reflect the fact that it's also home to movies and TV shows.

It followed up with the App Store soon after launching the iPhone, and then along came the iBookstore and Newsstand. Newsstand is now home to more than 5,000 different magazines and newspapers from right around the world. The stores are predictable, safe, and easy to use. No wonder they're so successful.

How to: Buy a magazine

Much like iBooks, Newsstand is
tied to its own dedicated store,
which uses the same Apple ID
that you use to download apps to
authorise and pay for magazine
and newspaper downloads.
Get started by tapping the
Store button on the top of the
Newsstand shelves.

All Newsstand publications
will work in a slightly different
way, depending on the software
that the publisher used to put
it together. Here we're going to
buy a copy of UK technology title,
MacUser. This is served using a
system developed by PixelMags,
so everything that holds true for
this title should also work with
others that use the same system.

Newsstand publications
are technically applications;
Newsstand itself is just a clever
convention Apple introduced
when it rolled out iOS 5 to
smarten up the process of
buying, reading and managing
them, and saving us from having
countless publications littering
our home screens.

Each one has a dedicated
page, just like an app (above)
detailing any special features,
such as interactive content,
and giving you a preview of the
current edition. Each app is a
container for all of the issues of
that title that you buy, so you'll
only ever see one cover on your
Newsstand shelves, no matter
how many back issues you own.

Once downloaded, your free
magazine app will appear on
your Newsstand shelves. Just
like regular apps, Newsstand
publications keep an eye on the
store and inform you when a new
issue is available by strapping
NEW across the corner of the
magazine cover thumbnail.

Most publishers allow you
to re-download old editions of

magazines you have already bought, so will ask you to set up an account through which they can log your purchases. If this is the first time you have bought a magazine from a publisher, you can create your account when you open the downloaded magazine app for the first time. If you already have an account, you'll be asked to log in, instead.

You're now ready to start downloading magazines. The app will present you with a list of available issues, accompanied by their prices and dates of publication. There will also often be options for subscribing for

one, three, six or 12 months, which in this instance are detailed by tapping the Subscribe button. For the moment, though, we just want to download a single issue. We have chosen the 26 October 2012 edition of MacUser. Tapping the price asks us to confirm that we want to buy it, just as the App Store does when we download an application. In this particular magazine app we can track the progress of the download on a drop-down Downloads dialogue (above left) through which we can also cancel the download, or repeat it if there was a problem. When the download completes

we just need to tap the cover to open it.

Our downloaded magazine looks just the same as the printed version (above), but because it's digital it has a few extra features. Tapping on the screen calls up a strip of thumbnails across the bottom of the pages, allowing us to preview the laid-out spreads and skip straight to the one we want. We can also drop down a list of contents from the toolbar at the top of the screen. The double-ended arrow, meanwhile, lets us loan our copy of this magazine to another user for up to four days.

Reminders

Never forget another important task

Reminders is a deceptively simple application. At first glance it appears to be nothing more than a simple list taker, giving you somewhere to jot down thoughts and reminders so that you don't need to worry about forgetting them.

Dig deeper, though, and you'll see that it's actually far more accomplished.

Reminders lets you set deadlines by which your jobs must be completed, and you can set priorities to help you keep tabs on what are your most important tasks.

On some devices, such as the iPhone or Mac, you can also set geographical reminders, although sadly these haven't yet been implemented on the iPad mini or full-sized iPad. If they had been, your iPad would be able to pop up a reminder when it spotted that you had arrived at or left a particular location where a task needed to be performed.

Reminders runs on all recent iOS devices and, as a bonus, works with OS X 10.8 Mountain Lion, too, which means it provides complete coverage for Apple-centric users, whichever platform they happen to be using at the time. That means that you can set up your reminders on your Mac, if you have one, safe in the knowledge that even if you're not at your desk when they come due they'll still pop up in your pocket on an iPhone, or on your iPad or iPad mini.

Over the next four pages we'll show you how to set new reminders and organise your tasks to stay productive.

Quick tip: timezones

If you're going to be travelling across different time zones, make sure you keep your iPad mini's clock set to the correct time if you need Reminders to pop up at times relevant to your current location.

You can set the clock's time zone by tapping Settings | General | Time & Date and switching Set Automatically to OFF, then tapping on the Time Zone line and typing the name of a large city nearby.

Review your list of Reminders frequently, rather than simply relying on the pop up alerts, so that you can clear out completed tasks and maintain a clearer view of the jobs that still await your attention.

Organising your reminders

By default, Reminders organises your jobs according to the lists on which they appear. There are two pre-set lists: Completed and Reminders. When you first start to use it, the jobs you enter will be sent directly to the Reminders list.

Should you have a specific project that you are working on and you want to hive off the tasks related to just that job so that you can find them quickly without having to tawl through each of your other commitments, tap the Create New List... line in the left-hand panel on the Reminders home screen and type in a name for your new list (see below). You can then switch between your two lists and keep your jobs separate from one another.

With multiple lists set up, you need to decide where each task should be filed. This is done in retrospect after you have saved the task by tapping its name in the main Reminders area (the lighter panel), followed by Show More... and then List. Select its destination from the options that appear, and then tap Done.

When you have completed one of your tasks, tap the check box beside its name on the reminder list to mark it as done.

Now tap the Completed list in the sidebar and you'll see that your accomplished job has automatically been moved to this new list, and when you return to the original list it has disappeared. This lets you keep a track of what you have accomplished over time and helps you see what still needs to be actioned.

If you want to delete a completed task entirely, tap its entry on the Completed list, followed by the Delete button on the pop-out tab, which you can see above, or slide a finger across the task and tap the Delete button at the end of the line.

Synchronising reminders

Reminders works across both iOS and OS X, which means you can synchronise your tasks across the Mac and iPad mini. Set up synchronisation on the iPad mini by tapping Settings | Reminders | Sync and choosing the time period that should be synchronised between the two platforms. You'll need a free iCloud account.

On the Mac, open System Preferences on OS X 10.8 Mountain Lion and click the iCloud icon. If you are running the correct version of the operating system you'll see an option for Calendars & Reminders (see left). Make sure this is ticked.

On the PC you can synchronise your reminders with Outlook. Download the iCloud Control Panel from http://support.apple.com/kb/DL1455.

How to: Set up a time-based reminder

[1] Use the '+' button at the top of the interface to start work on your first one, and press Return at the end of entering each one. This immediately takes you to the next line so you can start entering the next one without tapping '+' again. Tap anywhere else on the interface after entering your last one.

[2] Let's start adding some deadlines. We have created a task that tells us to back up our computer, so we'll tap this task, followed by the ON/OFF slider beside On a Day, then use the tumblers, dragging them up and down to select a date and time by which the job must be done.

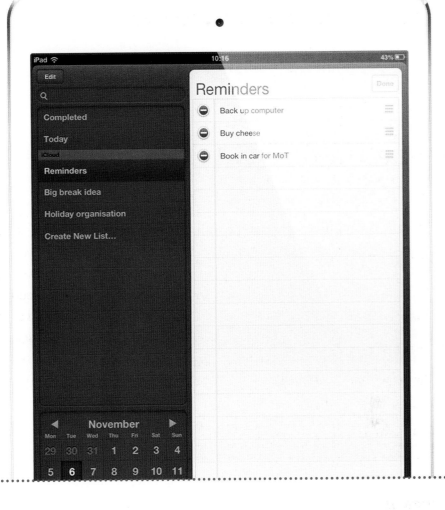

Organising tasks

Tasks are organised with the oldest at the top of the list and the newest at the bottom. If you want to promote a new job to the top of the list, tap the Edit button in the upper right corner of the main Reminders window and then drag your tasks into a new, more convenient order by holding your finger on the triple horizontal bars to the right of each one. Tapping the bars to the left deletes them.

[3] Backing up your computer is a very important job, so we'll give it a priority, too. We do this by tapping Done to return to the main settings page, followed by More and Priority. Here, we'll select High from the list of options so set it to the most urgent status.

[4] Before backing up we need to buy storage. We can remind ourselves to do this without creating a whole new reminder on the main screen by tapping within the Notes field and tapping in our reminder. This lets us annotate any jobs that aren't immediately obvious from their titles.

Siri

Your personal digital assistant

Siri is Apple's personal assistant. It first appeared on iPhone 4S, but with the introduction of iOS 6 it is now also found on the iPhone 5, Retina iPad and, to a slightly limited degree, the iPod touch announced in September 2012 alongside the iPhone 5. It also appears in the iPad mini, despite it sharing many hardware components with the iPad 2, with which Siri doesn't work.

As well as searching the web for answers to your questions, Siri can be used to input data into core iOS apps, like Calendar.

Siri conception

Apple didn't actually invent Siri. It was initially developed by Siri Inc – hence the name – and sold through the iOS App Store. Apple saw the genius in the application, and how useful it could be in advancing the iPhone's hands-free features, and snapped up the company and development team. It took Siri development in house, cancelled any existing plans to port the technology to competing BlackBerry and Android platforms and eventually took the service offline entirely in the run up to the launch of the iPhone 4S.

At the same time it was building an impressive data centre in Maiden, North Carolina, that would form the backbone of its online services, including iCloud and Siri, and when the iPhone 4S launched in late 2011 it was with Siri firmly in place, providing web services and impressively accurate dictation tools to all.

However, it wasn't perfect. It only supported four languages at launch – English, German, French

Siri understands

When it launched as part or the iPhone 4S, Siri understood only English, French, German and Japanese, but with the introduction of enhanced features in iOS 6 support has now been increased to cover nine languages:

- English
- French
- German
- Japanese
- Spanish
- Italian
- Korean
- Mandarin
- Cantonese

and Japanese – and performance outside of the United States was variable as it hadn't been fully localised to know about national traffic systems and businesses.

Siri today

That second factor is still true to a degree. Siri's performance

Hold the Home button to call up the floating Siri window

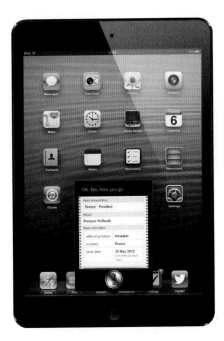

is still better inside the United States than anywhere else in the world, although Apple is adding new features to the coverage it gives for international users over time so the longer you use it, the more you'll find it useful as more of your questions get answers.

Further, it has expanded the range of languages in which Siri can understand requests and provide answers to nine, and now caters for the Italian and Chinese markets. The latter is particularly important as Apple looks to become a dominant mobile force in that country.

Siri's personality

Siri is very personable and has his or her own personality (Siri's gender varies from country to country, depending on who is providing the voice). This allows him or her to carry on a conversation with you, where one question can draw on the results of an earlier request. So, you could ask 'Who is the president of France?' and when Siri gives you an answer it would understand that a following question along the lines of 'how old is he' still relates to the French leader (see above left).

How do I use Siri?

Siri doesn't assume any technical expertise on your part. You don't even need to type anything to use it; it's all controlled by your voice. Neither do you need to learn any arcane instructions or

commands: you just talk to it in plain English.

If you've seen Star Trek you'll know how the crew of the Enterprise talk to their onboard computer in plain English. Siri works in a similar fashion.

You start by holding down the Home button until the Siri icon appears at the bottom of the screen (see above). It looks like a silver button with a microphone in the middle. Speak your command, such as 'what will the weather be like tomorrow', or 'remind me to phone home on Friday morning' and wait for an answer.

Siri will pass your command back to Apple's data centre where the remote voice recognition applications will analyse the sound wave and pull out recognised words and phrases. These will be further analysed to discern their meaning and then used as the basis of

47

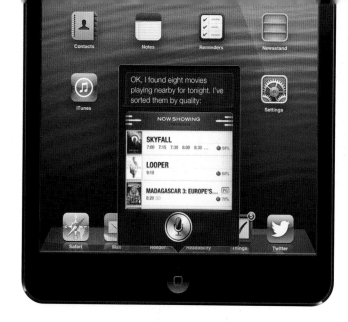

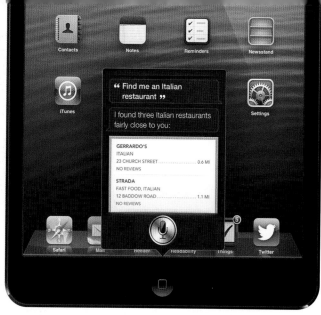

Siri has access to the iPad mini's Location Services features, which means it can help you plan a complete night out by calling up suggestions and make recommendations for things to do, places to eat and places to stay close to where you are at the point of interrogation.

your query. If it was a request for information it will do its best to answer it with reference to online databases and the web. If it was an instruction or a command that can be performed by your iPad mini, it is passed back to the device and the relevant local application takes over from there.

Unlike early Mac- and PC-based voice recognition tools,

you don't need to give Siri any training before you start using it, as it's being trained and improved all the time because it's being used by so many people around the world simultaneously.

When it first launched it had some trouble with some regional accents including, famously, some Scottish voices, but Apple claims that as more people interact with Siri and it learns how to interpret what they say this should become less of an issue.

What can Siri tell me?

Siri works by hooking into a range of online databases, but the information that it pulls out

Siri answers common questions with referenced data. Here it has provided us with the week's weather forecast just because we asked about the temperature.

of them and its relevance to your queries depends very much on the country from which you're accessing them. In general, though, Siri has a good general knowledge and can tailor the information that it passes back to be relevant to your local area.

For example, you could ask 'will it be cold tomorrow?' and Siri will check the local forecast. Because your iPad mini has various location-detecting tools built in to the operating system (and an integrated GPS receiver in the cell-enabled version) it already knows where you're located, so doesn't need you to specify '...in Edinburgh' or '... in Paris' to give you the correct information.

However, tacking that kind of location onto the end of your request will allow you to look up information relevant to places where you aren't currently standing.

More generalised requests could simply lead to globally-relevant answers, such as 'how many grams are there in a pound'.

Some information is patchy or simply unavailable outside of the United States at the time of writing. For example, traffic conditions work well inside the US but aren't available in the United Kingdom. Likewise, when iOS 6 was announced Apple simultaneously announced that Siri would be able to provide American Football sports results, but didn't announce an equivalent feature for UK-based football teams playing what US users would call 'soccer'. Over time this is likely to change as Siri's repertoire improves.

Using Siri with other iOS applications

Some Siri requests don't require that the servers pass back the answer to a question, but that they instruct a core iOS application to perform a function.

For example, you can text people directly by saying 'text Alan I am running five minutes late' (Alan's contact details would be pulled out of the Contacts app), or you could set an appointment in your diary by telling Siri 'remind me that it's Alan's birthday on Monday'. Because you had specified no time, Siri would enter this as a whole-day event.

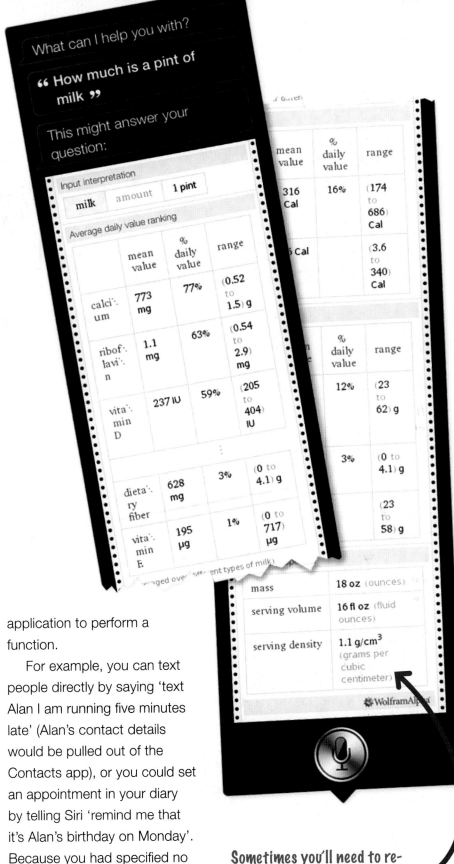

Sometimes you'll need to re-phrase your question to get the answer you're after. Here, we just wanted the cost of milk.

Maps

A more tactile way to explore the world around you

The Maps application has had an complete overhaul in iOS 6. Previously the iPad's native navigation tool had drawn down its cartographic data from Google Maps, but as Apple moves away from using Google services (the YouTube app has also disappeared in this latest release of the operating system) it has switched it out for its own online mapping system.

For the end user this shouldn't make too big a difference. You can still switch between different map types, including a regular plan view and satellite imagery, you can check on the traffic and plan a route by car and foot. Some of the results can be a little hit and miss, and Apple is working hard to improve things, but in these early days you may need to cut it a little slack. Other than that, though, just about the only thing missing is Google Street View.

It still ties in with other iPad mini applications, too, providing mapping and location services to third-party add-ons, and helping you plot your colleagues' details from the Contacts application or addresses in their emails.

Browsing

Unless you've moved it into a folder, Maps is found on the iPad mini home screen, and each time you launch it, it will pick up from wherever you last left off. The best way to get to know it is to simply browse around. Drag your finger across the screen to pull the map in any direction. After taking a moment to stream the next section from the Internet it will update to show you the settlements, roads and named businesses in the newly-uncovered area.

Try zooming in by placing two fingers on the screen and slowly drawing them apart, then do the same in reverse, pinching them together to zoom out.

Street plans are only half of the story. As the Maps application takes its data from a centralised server, it also has access to high

Switching between different views lets you choose from a regular drawn plan or satellite photography, optionally with info overlays.

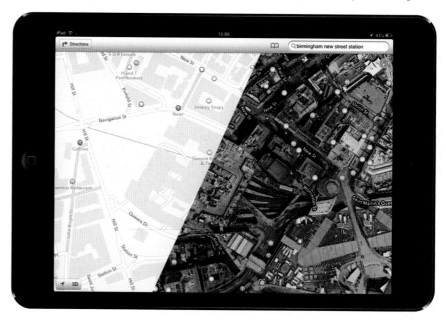

iOS 6 introduced a new 3D view to Maps, which wraps raised representations of the buildings in a scene with realistic surfaces and textures. Dragging on the screen flies around the scene.

resolution aerial photography for much of the world, and this can also be streamed to the iPad mini, then scrolled, zoomed and searched in exactly the same way. To switch between the two, tap the button in the lower right corner of the interface with the curling paper icon to call up the underlying menu, which lets you pick between standard, hybrid or satellite. You can see the difference between them

to the left, which demonstrates the standard and hybrid views. Satellite view simply drops the hybrid view's text overlays.

Hybrid overlays the standard plan-style map over the downloaded aerial photography so you can see not only the buildings and geographic features on the ground but also labels showing where they are. The hybrid view is particularly clever, as not only does it allow you to

re-size the photography while keeping the maps proportionally accurate, but it will also intelligently tailor the amount of information shown on the maps to avoid blotting out the photography.

So, when you're at city level rather than building level it will show only the major arteries instead of every single road, and change the size of the font used to label them so that it remains legible. This way you can use a wide area overview to get yourself to more or less the right location before zooming to a more appropriate scale when you need to start navigating individual roads.

iOS 6 introduces proper 3D views to the satellite maps. Available on the iPhone 4S and 5, and the iPad and iPad mini, this feature is called Flyover, and it renders the centres of important cities fully so you can see how the buildings relate to one another. Twisting your fingers on the screen lets you turn them around. Dragging lets you fly across them, while sliding your fingers up and down opposite sides of the screen lets you change the angle of slant from which you're viewing the selected scene.

Searching

You can't spend your whole life dragging a map around. It would be like taping together every Ordnance Survey sheet and then carefully folding and re-folding them every time you wanted to look at a different part of the country. It's far better to jump straight to the map you want, in both the paper- and pixel-based worlds, by searching.

Tap inside the input box and enter a search query. This can be very specific or quite general; it understands landmarks as well as addresses. For example, White House, Washington DC, will take you straight there for a view that is best seen using satellite imagery rather than the plain old map. Likewise, 30 Cleveland Street, London, UK, will accurately pinpoint the home of Dennis Publishing, at which point we would recommend switching back to the map view.

But what if you're out and about and you desperately need a local service? That's when

Many large cities have been rendered in 3D form. To view photorealistic renders of places you know, switch to satellite view and then use the buildings button in the lower left corner.

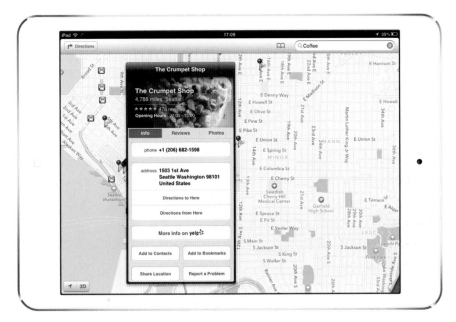

Searching for a business by name or service type calls up a series of matches that fall within the current view. Tapping on one of the pushpins that mark the results calls up full contact details.

searching with business types comes to the fore. Imagine you're in Seattle, the home of coffee, and need a caffeine hit to start the day. Tap in the search box and type coffee, and a volley of pins will drop onto the map, each one of which marks out a different outlet.

Tapping one brings up its name on an attached tag, on the end of which you'll see a small arrow in a circle. Tap the arrow and the floating box expands to reveal that outlet's contact details, giving you the address, phone number, email details, website and other supplementary information (see above).

Where am I?

An easier way to see exactly where you are, which is particularly handy if you are in the middle of a large city, is to use the self-positioning tool. Tap the compass pointer icon in the bottom-left corner of the screen and the map will re-centre and be overlaid with a blue circle. Your position will be within that ring.

The cellular iPad mini will primarily use GPS to get a fix on your position, if possible. GPS works by receiving a stream of data from a constellation of satellites orbiting the planet. These satellites transmit a time

code alongside details of their current position. The iPad mini looks at the time codes and compares their accuracy. By working out how much they differ, it can work out how long it took the time codes to reach it from each satellite, and thus how far away the receivers are. When it has a fix on two or more satellites (the more the better) it can then draw a virtual line from each one, and where they converge will always be your position.

If the iPad mini can't get a perfect fix on the satellites, perhaps because of cloud cover, trees overhead or the fact that it's inside a building, it augments this information with supplementary data received from the cellphone network, various public Wi-Fi networks and your own personal network. Together these provide supplementary triangulation information that enable it to estimate your current location. This same supplementary technology works on the iPad mini without cellular features, which lacks the required GPS receiver chip.

How to: Plan a route using Maps

Searching is only half of the story. It's no good finding a coffee shop you want to visit if you don't then know how to get there. Fortunately the Maps app has a set of very accomplished route planning tools that can help in this respect, giving you street-by-street and turn-by-turn directions with a high level of accuracy for towns and cities all over the world.

Most of your route planning will almost certainly be done with reference to private transport on public roads. However, when tapping in the start and end points of your route you can also select from foot or public transport by tapping the mode buttons above the start and end boxes. At the time of writing, coverage of pedestrian routes was good, but public transport options directed you to the App Store.

If you would find it easier to follow a list of written directions that you can scroll, rather than stepping point by point through a map, then tap the Overview button at the top of the screen, followed by the button with three lines on it at the bottom. This opens a list of written directions with turn signs on each line.

You can now drag the list up and down to see what's coming up around the next corner. If you want to see how the layout of the road relates to each step, choose the one you want to examine and tap on it to switch back to the map view.

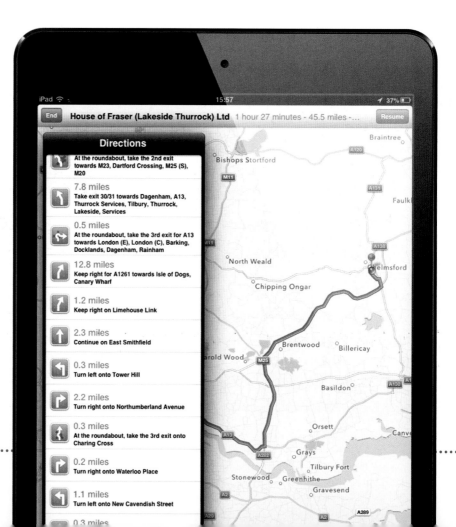

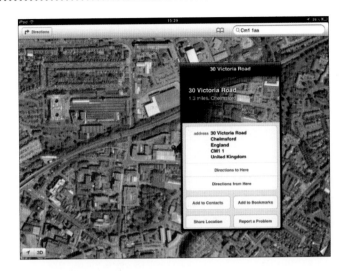

[1] Either tap the location finder if you want to navigate from your current position, or search for a location in the regular way. Tap on the marker that shows the result, followed by the blue arrow to see the contact details sheet. Pick Directions from Here.

[2] This location will be automatically entered into one half of the directions equation. All you need do now is enter your destination into the other half of the pair. Do this and then tap Return.

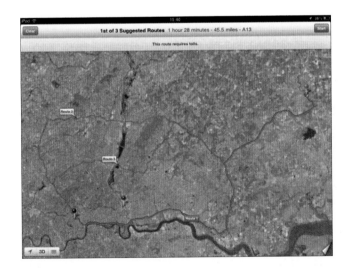

[3] Maps draws up a selection of routes for your journey. You can tap between them to see how they differ, but you should always find that Route 1 is the shortest in terms of time taken, if not actual miles travelled. Tap the one you want to follow.

[4] Pick the route you want to use and then tap the start button. Your iPad mini zooms to the first step of the journey. When you have completed that instruction, swipe left to reveal the next one. Continue working your way through the journey or, better, travel with a companion who can do this for you so that you can keep your eyes on the road.

iBooks
Your complete digital library

Apple wants us all to stop buying bound pages and switch instead to digital reading. It's not the first company to have this idea, as the likes of Sony (with the Reader) and Amazon (with the Kindle) already have competing products. Indeed, Amazon is now encroaching on Apple's own territory with the Kindle Fire and Kindle Fire HD, its Android-based tablet devices.

Of course, iBooks in itself probably isn't enough to entice anyone to buy an iPad mini. Apple's interest, then, more likely lies more in selling content, and to that end it has developed its own iBookstore, which works along very similar lines to the App Store and iTunes Store and can also be accessed on the iPad mini using the same Apple ID login credentials.

iBooks organises your reading material on a series of shelves, split into collections so that you can easily find exactly the book you're after. Tapping the Store button spins around the shelves to reveal an online bookshop.

iBooks App

iBooks isn't installed by default, but it's a free download from the App Store. The first time you launch the App Store application you'll be prompted to download this and a host of other apps, including the Podcast application, iTunes U and both Find Friends and Find iPhone.

Once up and running, your books are arranged on shelves, a little like the albums in the Music application (see below). Tapping one opens it on the screen in your choice of font and text size.

This is managed through the font setting dialogue that hides behind the AA button at the top of each page (see right). Tap this and choose between smaller and larger characters in seven common fonts. The slider above this controls the brightness of the display so that you can tailor it to your own particular eyes and the lighting conditions around you, while Themes lets you set the colours used. iBooks 3, the latest revision, which shipped on the same day as the iPad mini, now lets you scroll books from the very first word to the last without

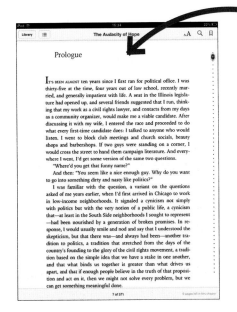

Tap the AA button to call up the text and theme options, the latter of which includes iBooks 3's continuous scrolling view

Below: one advantage of digital reading is that your books are fully searchable, allowing you to pinpoint information more quickly than you can in print.

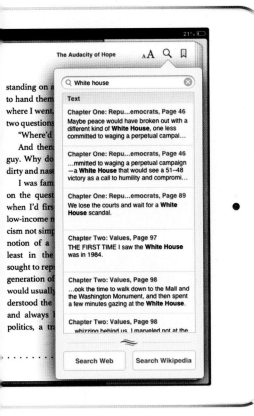

any breaks for distinct pages, as though they were laid out like a regular web page.

To the right of both of these is a picture of a magnifying glass, which signifies the search tool (see below). Tap this and enter your search term and it will hunt through the book you're reading to find every instance of that word combination. If it remains ambiguous, Search Web and Search Wikipedia buttons at the bottom of the results panel let you search online.

Each time you open a book, iBooks remembers where you last left off, so you shouldn't ever lose your place, and if you're on the contents page of a book you'll see a Resume button at the top of the page that, when tapped, takes you to your last-opened page. However, you can also set bookmarks throughout the text by simply tapping the bookmark logo in the top right corner of any page (if you can't see this, briefly tap the main body of the screen to call up the iBooks toolbar). You can set several bookmarks in this way and they will all be organised

on the Bookmarks page of the book's index page.

The longer you use iBooks, the more you'll fall in love with this way of reading, with a progress bar at the bottom of the screen showing how far through the book you have read, and the integrated dictionary ensuring you are never lost for words.

Taking notes

iBooks is a great learning tool, allowing you to carry a whole library of books wherever you go and use spare moments to revise. To help you keep note of important sections, iBooks has an in-built highlighting tool.

To use it, hold your finger on the screen to select one of the words from your selection, then release it. Drag the spots at either end of the selection to enlarge it so that it encompasses the whole of the section you want to include, and then select Highlight from the pop-up menu that appears above the selection.

Highlights are also stored in the app's Bookmarks section.

Alternative outlets

Although the iBookstore is built in to iBooks, there's nothing to stop you buying unprotected ePub books elsewhere on your Mac or PC, dragging them in to iTunes and then synchronising them to your iPad mini.

How to: buy books from the iBookstore

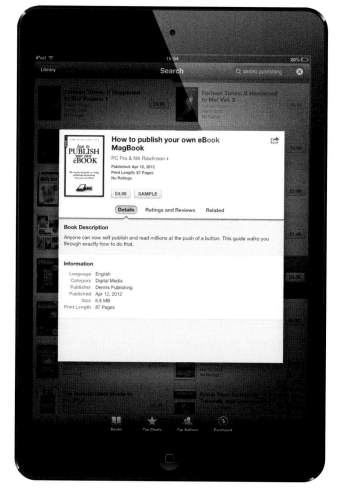

[1] Open iBooks and tap the Store button on the toolbar at the top of the application. The app flips around to reveal the Store hiding behind it as though it was a secret doorway. Use the different options on the toolbar at the foot of the app to check out the charts, browse categories or search for a book by author name, title or keyword.

[2] The store index is extensive, and it's easy to find almost any book you're after. Bear in mind, though, that not every book published in print is available in the iBookstore. Likewise, not every book available digitally is also available in print. When you've found the book you want, tap SAMPLE to download the first few pages for free.

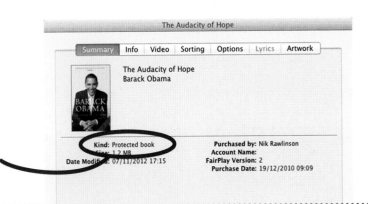

Apple applies the same kind of copy protection to eBooks as it does to apps. You can check whether a book is protected by selecting it in iTunes and picking Info from the File menu

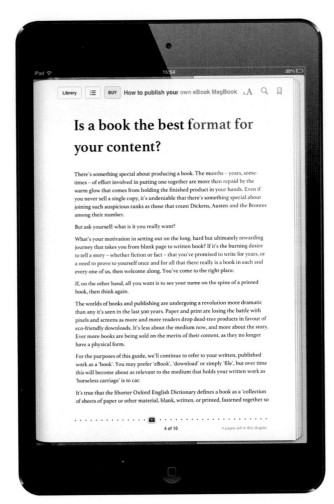

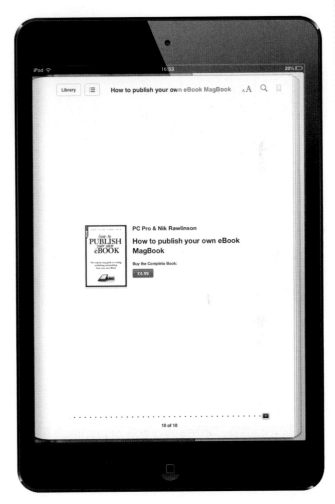

[3] The sample is delivered to your shelves, with a 'SAMPLE' strap slashed across one corner so you know at a glance that it's not the complete volume. Tap it to read the contents and audition the book. Samples are generally fairly generous, so you can get a good idea of the writing style and thrust of the story or, for non-fiction, the subject matter.

[4] When you get to the end of the sample, you're shown a button to download the complete volume, at which point you'll be charged. If you don't want the rest of the book, you can keep the sample for free. If you enjoyed the book you don't need to get this far before splashing out as a BUY button appears at the top of every page.

Music
Audible entertainment wherever you are

Don't confuse the Music and iTunes applications. On your desktop or laptop computer, you'd use iTunes to listen to your music as well as to buy new content, including apps, videos and TV shows. On the iPad mini, on the other hand, (and all other iOS devices) the iTunes app is only ever used for downloading content. The Music application is where you'll turn to listen to your music collection, whether bought directly or synchronised from your Mac or PC.

Despite this, Music bears more than a passing resemblance to iTunes on a regular computer. Across the top of the screen you'll see a set of familiar transport controls for playing back your music, fast forwarding, rewinding, changing volume and so on. Below this you'll see your tracks. If you have relevant artwork for all of your albums, they will be displayed like albums on a shelf, or books in the iBooks application. Tapping on the cover of an album flips it over so that you can see a list of its tracks.

Music shares several visual cues with the iTunes application on a Mac or PC, with album art and category-based sorting.

Below the albums and track names in your library are buttons that let you change the main display to sort your content by song name, artist name, album, genre or composer (see above). All of the data attached to your tracks that makes this possible is transferred at the same time as your music if you're filling your iPad mini from a Mac or PC, or downloaded at the same time as your purchases if you're buying content from the iTunes Store. If you're ripping an existing

CD-based music collection to your computer's iTunes library it therefore makes sense to spend time making sure the track names are accurate.

The easiest way to find a track is to use the search box. As you type, it will trim the list of results in the window below. It also greys out some of the buttons at the bottom of the screen to leave only those categories in which your results appear. The longer you type, the more of these will disappear, but if you still have

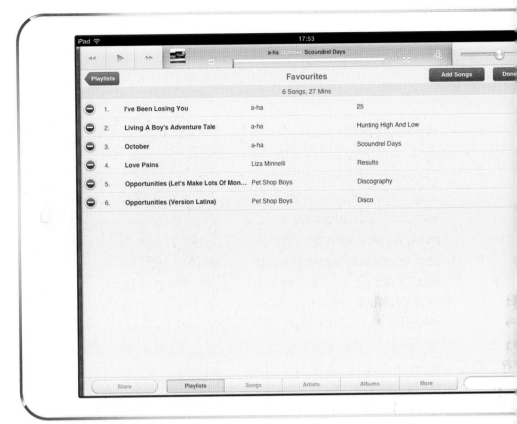

more than one in full black text, you can tap between them to filter out those items that don't meet your requirements.

Building playlists

Although the library looks quite sparse when you first start using Music on the iPad mini, you can build it up by creating playlists in which to organise your tracks. Tap the Playlists button, followed by New, and enter a name for your playlist, then to populate it tap the elements you want to include. Again, use the category buttons at the bottom of the screen to switch between artists, albums and so on, selecting tracks from each one. When picking tracks from an album, tap the album's cover art and it will flip over to show you a track listing from which you can select the tracks you want to include.

The easy alternative

If you don't have the time or the inclination to build your own playlist, then why not ask your

The most efficient means of organising a large library is to sort your tracks into playlists. Editing a playlist lets you add and remove further tracks, with the red bars to the left deleting them from the list, but leaving them in the library itself.

iPad mini to do it for you? Beside the volume slider at the top of the screen you'll see what looks like some neutrons spinning around each other. This is the Genius button. Genius builds playlists of tracks that go well together based on information submitted anonymously by the millions of iTunes users around the world.

Tap it and select a starting track, and Music will build a playlist of 25 songs based on an

algorithm that deduces which tracks go well together. If you don't like them, tap Refresh or, if you think they're perfect, opt for Save to store the list for future.

If you have any trouble creating Genius playlists, make sure the Genius feature is enabled by connecting your iPad mini to your Mac or PC, starting iTunes there and checking the option to turn on this feature, then synchronise your device.

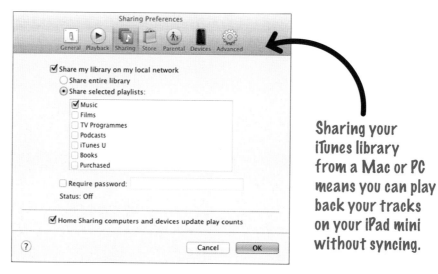

Shared playlists

If you're using your iPad mini at home or work and you also keep a regular iTunes library there, enable Home Sharing on both your iPad and your Mac or PC. You'll then be able to play your full library on your iPad mini without syncing it first. To share a library, open iTunes on your regular computer and click iTunes | Preferences... | Sharing on the Mac, or Edit | Preferences | Sharing on the PC.

Check the box beside Share my library on my local network. Your library, complete with its playlists, will then appear in the sidebar of any other installation of iTunes running on your network. By default, each user will see the whole of your library.

Despite sharing your library in this way, you retain a great degree of control over what can be seen within it.

If you don't want to share the more embarrassing sections of your iTunes library, you need only gather them into a dedicated playlist and click on

the radio button beside 'Share selected playlists', then check only the playlists you want to share – remembering to omit that collection of hidden tracks that you don't want to make public.

You can also restrict the people who are able to access any of your library by setting a password. This is particularly useful if you're running an older

Mac or PC that might become bogged down if too many other users start playing music – or shared TV shows and movies – from your computer.

To access the shared tracks, simply tap More on the toolbar, followed by Shared. Pick the name of your shared home library and all of its tracks will appear as though they were local.

Sharing your iTunes library from a Mac or PC means you can play back your tracks on your iPad mini without syncing.

Explore your albums

You might not think the album view is particularly informative, showing only a grid of your imported or downloaded albums, but it is actually a great piece of design, allowing you to quickly glance across your library to get a feel for what's available, and then tap your chosen album to flip it around and see the tracks that it contains. Each one is listed in order, with a track number, name and length, while the currently playing track – if it appears on the selected album – is marked out with a small play triangle in place of its track number.

To step out of the track listing and return to the album overview screen, tap the grey title bar, or anywhere on the screen away from the tracks.

Enjoy your cover art

It seems such a shame when you have a 7.9in screen at your disposal to only ever view your album art in the grid view or as a thumbnail beside the progress bar when you're playing back your music.

Tap that thumbnail and the art expands to fill the screen. Tapping it again overlays it with playback controls. At the top of the screen are volume, play, forwards and backwards. Beside these, the progress bar and, to the right the regular volume control. At the bottom of the screen you'll see the regular sorting buttons, which when tapped will return you to a view of your library. The left-pointing chevron, meanwhile, steps back to the album track listing.

Build a genius playlist

If you don't want to follow our instructions for building a defined playlist you can assign the task to the Music app. Tap the genius button on the playback bar and select a track from your library.

Your iPad mini will examine all of the other tracks in your collection and pick out a list of other tracks that it considers work well alongside it. To do this it uses information submitted anonymously by the millions of iPod, Music and iTunes users around the world, which is analysed centrally and accessed by the iTunes and Music applications. As well as the current track you can see which tracks the Music app has queued, allowing you to skip straight to a favourite entry.

Videos
Movies and TV shows on the move

Videos is one of the simplest apps on the iPad mini. Many of its features were at one time rolled into the now defunct iPod application, which itself was replaced by 'Music'.

Videos exists purely to play back downloads from the iTunes Store, or movies and TV shows you've synchronised through iTunes from your Mac or PC. Movies that you shoot yourself using third party applications and the built-in camera on your iPad mini are stored instead in your regular photo albums, while those that you edit with an application like iMovie are stored in the app itself until you synchronise or send them to a third-party online service, or actively choose to save them out to your Photo roll.

Your videos are organised into collections, with related episodes gathered into parent groups, each of which includes details of how many episodes it contains. You'll also see a small blue indicator beside the name of each episode showing whether a programme is new (filled in blue),

partially watched (half-filled with blue) or watched right through (empty). The same indicator appears in the overview of each of your collections showing you how many of the constituent videos you still need to watch inside it.

The controls are simple, and if you have any familiarity with a regular DVD player then you'll already know what they do.

Unfortunately there's no way to find related movies from the playback half of the app, as there was with the now defunct YouTube application, but if you step back to a list of TV shows

inside any one of your collections you'll find a link to Get More Episodes... which takes you directly to the iTunes Store.

Apple maintains an extensive library of both films and TV shows in its store, which you can download directly onto your iPad mini. With most series you can choose standard and high definition videos, the latter of which cost more, and you can buy either single episodes or a complete series. If you have set up iCloud to synchronise your purchases, anything you buy on your iPad mini will simultaneously appear on your Mac or PC.

How to: Add movies and TV shows to your library

You can buy movies and TV shows directly through the iTunes App. Apple provides a range of recommendations on the home screen, but using the Search function will let you explore the library in more depth. If you're contemplating viewing a film that you probably won't watch more than once, then rent it instead of buying it and save yourself some money.

You can often choose between high definition and standard definition content for both TV shows and films. You'll find SD and HD buttons at the top of their listings if that's the case. Tapping the buttons lets you switch between them and changes the price as appropriate.

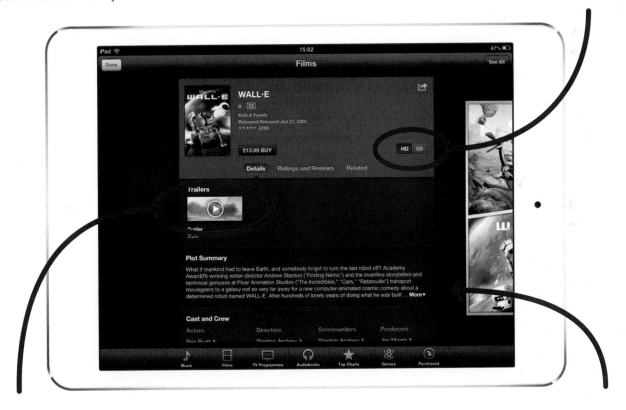

Once you've found the show you're after, tap its thumbnail to open the full listing. If you're looking at a film, you'll be able to play a preview clip to check it's what you want. If it's a TV show and you want to do the same, tap one of the episodes and you'll find the preview clip at the top of the screen.

Each programme and film is accompanied by a description, episode run-down, viewer reviews and related content that you might also enjoy once you've finished watching the content you're buying. They will also have star ratings if other viewers have provided them.

Podcasts

Tune in to radio and video from right around the world

Apple launched its dedicated Podcasts app shortly before shipping iOS 6, and when the new operating system was released to the general public it completed the process of removing podcasts from the iTunes and Music apps and transitioning everyone over to the new application. It works in a very similar way to iBooks and Newsstand, with an integrated store giving you access to an extensive library of podcasts ready to download for free.

The Podcasts application itself isn't installed at the point you unbox your iPad mini, but you will be prompted to download it for free the first time you fire up the App Store. If you previously skipped this step then don't worry: you can download it at a later date by searching for Podcasts.

If you've not come across them before, podcasts are recorded programmes, originally put out by amateurs but now widely adopted by professional broadcasters like the BBC, too.

The vast majority are audio-only, but there's a good selection – often called vodcasts – that also incorporate video.

There's some disagreement about where the name comes from, with some claiming that it relates to the iPod, and other stating that the POD part actually stands for 'Personal On Demand' casts.

The easiest way to get started with the Podcasts app is to browse the Top Stations tab (tap this on the bottom toolbar)

and dragging the subject areas at the top of the screen left and right to choose one. Each brings up a whole column of different podcasts that you can choose from by scrolling the column up and down (see image, below). Tap the switch at the top to choose audio or video.

Of course, this only brings up a subset of all the podcasts available online, so for a wider selection, check out the Podcasts store by tapping Store on the bottom toolbar.

How to: Subscribe to your favourite podcast

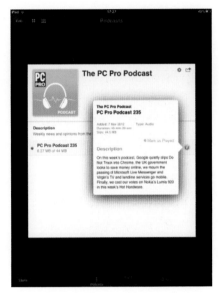

[1] Tap the Store button to enter the podcasts store (don't worry – despite what the name might suggest, everything there is free) and then use the search box to enter a keyword, broadcaster or the name of a podcast that you want to listen to. The app calls up a list of results in much the same way that the iBookstore lists matches to your searches there. Tap the icon beside any episode to call up the full details, including reviews, ratings and a list of related podcasts that you might find interesting.

[2] Tap the down-pointing arrow beside an episode to download it to your iPad mini. When it arrives it will be organised in your podcast library, which you can find by tapping the Podcasts button on the toolbar, beside Top Stations. Tap a podcast in this view to open the individual episodes. You can also tap the 'i' button to the right of any episode to find out what it contains. This is useful if you keep a back catalogue of old episodes and need help remembering where you heard something before.

[3] Tap an episode to listen to it, or tap the cog icon at the top of the details screen for its settings.

From here you can choose whether or not you want to subscribe to the podcast on an ongoing basis, in which case your iPad mini will automatically download new episodes as they become available, and how they should be organised. By default it sorts them with the newest at the top of the list, which is the most logical. Scrolling down from here, you can also mark all episodes either as played or unplayed.

iTunes

Your all in one music, movies and TV show store

Apple has never been afraid to strike out on its own. It doesn't use Windows, the world's most widely deployed consumer operating system, it has a tendency to drop legacy hardware from its products before anyone else, and in the early days of online music sales it quickly established itself as one of the biggest and most successful players.

In part that was because its store, managed through iTunes, was associated so closely with the world's most successful portable music player, the iPod, which continues to this day both in hardware form, and as software in the shape of the Music app. The iTunes app, on the other hand, is never used for playing back anything other than previews on iOS. Instead, it's a dedicated shop window for music, movies and TV shows you can download to your device.

How to: Download an album from iTunes

[1] The iTunes Store looks much like each of Apple's other shops, which received a refresh when the company shipped iOS 6. The homepage displays new releases, a free single of the week, and content that the iTunes Store editors are promoting at the point when you visit. If you don't see what you're looking for here, you'll need to go searching.

[2] There are several ways in which you can navigate the store. The buttons at the bottom of the screen switch between different media types, and those at the top select genres such as pop, dance, alternative and so on. The search box in the top corner can pinpoint a specific album, but we've tapped the 'Under £5' promotion on the front page.

Spotted something you think a friend would enjoy? Share a link with them direct from its listing in the iTunes Store

It uses the same login credentials as the Mac and Windows version, and even if you haven't got iCloud's automatic synchronisation feature turned on to make sure that content you download on one device is available on all the others, you can still download a free second copy of anything you've bought in the past by tapping the Purchased button at the bottom of the iTunes application interface, searching for the product and tapping the cloud icon to retrieve a new copy.

Of course, you don't have to download all your music this way; if you have a CD or DVD drive in your computer you can rip your existing CDs and transfer them via iTunes. Using the Store, though, guarantees reliable quality and easy transfers.

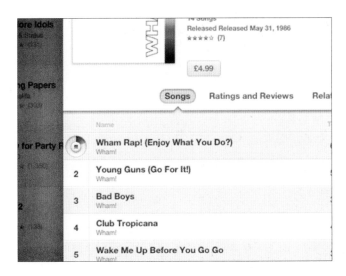

[3] Here we've tapped on the artwork for an album included in the offer. In much the same way that this spins around an album in the Music application, this has enlarged and reversed the entry in the iTunes Store so that we can see the individual tracks. We can buy them separately or tap on their titles, as we've done here, to preview each one.

[4] It's usually cheaper to buy a whole album rather than buying each track individually, so if you want to download the whole thing, tap the price, followed by the green BUY ALBUM that replaces it. If you have automatic downloads synchronised over iCloud, the same tracks will be downloaded to your other iOS devices and the iTunes library on your Mac or PC.

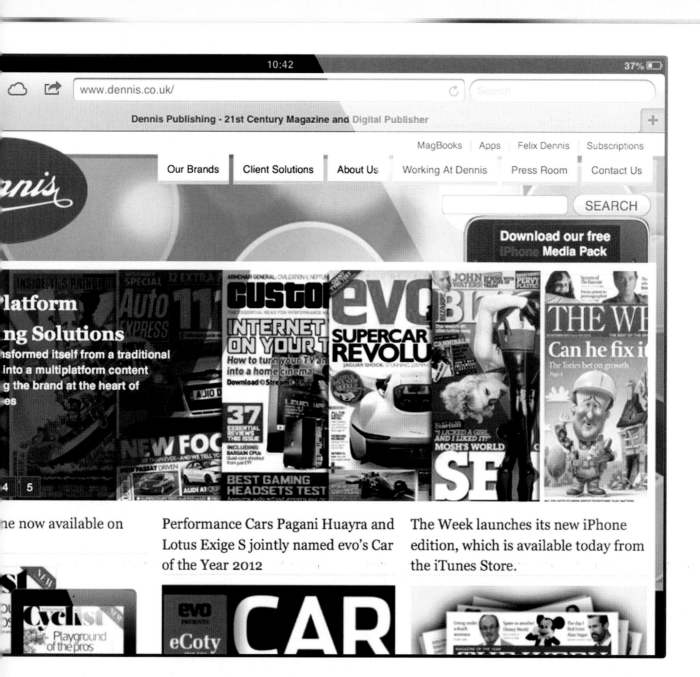

Chapter 3
Online

Mail

Helping you keep in touch while away from your desk

Apple learnt a lesson from the eponymous BlackBerry device when it was first developing its iPhone and iPad operating system: users like email on the move. We don't like having to wait until we get back home to catch up on gossip, notes and work messages, and neither do we want to wait to reply. Like the best students, Apple went out into the world and did better than its teacher.

Email on the iPad mini is far from a weak point. It has presets for Gmail (Google Mail),

Yahoo!, iCloud, AOL, Hotmail and Exchange, and also lets you manually add a regular Pop3 or Imap account from another provider. This last option, along with Exchange, will be of particular interest to business users, as it allows messages to be hosted on a central server rather than downloaded on an ad-hoc basis and deleted.

iCloud works in much the same way, allowing you to see your in- and out-boxes in the same state on an iPad mini, iPhone, Mac or PC, or through a web browser.

Adding your first email account

If you don't already have an email account that you would like to use with your iPad mini you can set up a free account with five of the pre-set services in the iPad mini's mail application by visiting the boxed sites on the opposite page using a regular web browser.

By far the most useful for any iPad mini user is iCloud, which provides you with a push email account. This transfers messages to the mini as soon as they are received, mimicking the BlackBerry's way of working and saving you from having to manually invoke a collection. It also provides you with a wholly memorable email address and can be used with other services such as iTunes Match and Find My iPhone/iPad to provide additional features.

iOS makes it very easy to add a range of widely-used email account types thanks to the presets in place on arrival.

Picking up messages

When first set up, your email will be set to only pick up when you tell it to. This is great for making sure you rule your messages, rather than allowing them to rule you, but it's not entirely convenient.

To set your iPad mini to poll the server and download new messages automatically, tap Settings | Mail, Contacts, Calendars | Fetch New Data and choose from every 15, 30 or 60 minutes, depending on how much of an email junkie you are (see below). Checking more frequently can run down

Setting your email to Push is the quickest way to receive new incoming messages, but if you need to slow things down then choose a different frequency.

Sign up for a free email account

There are plenty of options to choose from when it comes to picking an email account to use with your iPad mini. If you don't already have your own account or operate your own server, these services can help you get started.

iCloud	www.icloud.com
Yahoo! Mail	www.ymail.com
AOL Mail	www.aol.com
Google Mail	www.google.com/mail
Hotmail	www.hotmail.com

From iOS 6 onwards, you force Mail to check for new messages by dragging down the inbox beyond the uppermost item. As you continue to drag down, a lozenge appears, which stretches. At the point it snaps, iOS checks in with the server for new content.

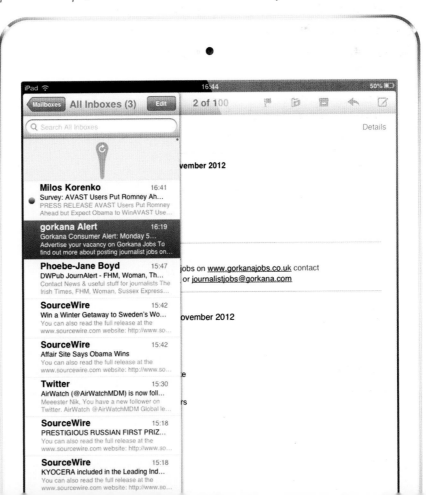

Save time by deleting emails based on their subject lines and previews by tapping Edit and selecting the messages to trash by tapping the lozenges in the left-hand margin

How to move and delete multiple messages

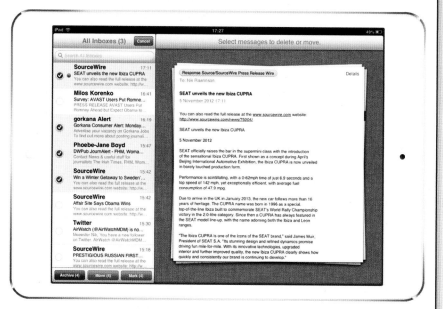

There are two ways to delete single messages from your inbox. You can either tap the trash icon on the menu bar or, if that's not present, swipe a single finger across the message header in the inbox listing in the left-hand column to call up the Delete or Archive button.

This isn't a practical solution if you need to delete a lot of emails at once, though, as it would take you far too long to step through each one. Fortunately, though, there is a simple way to delete several messages at once and save yourself a lot of swiping and tapping.

Look at the top of your message list for the Edit button (step back into your inbox if you can only see the list of your mailboxes in the left-hand column).

Tap this button and all of your messages will shift to the right to make space for a column of lozenges. As you tap each one – and you can tap more than one

in sequence – you will select the message beside it. You can then delete the selected messages by tapping the red delete button at the foot of the column.

Notice how every message that you've selected to delete is stacked up in the right-hand window so that you can preview it before wiping it from your iPad. If you change your mind about removing one from your mailbox, tap its lozenge in the left-hand panel for a second time to clear it, and it will be removed from the

deletion stack. This works even if the message is not displayed on the top of the stacked queue.

If you don't want to delete the messages, but instead move them to another mailbox, tap the Move button at the bottom of the column and you will be returned to the overall mailbox view. Here, tap on the mailbox into which you want to move the selected messages. See the text opposite for a quicker way to move just one message at a time between mailboxes on your iPad.

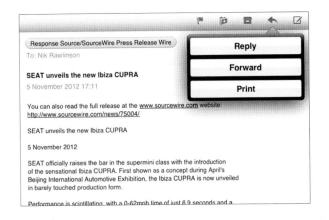

The Mail toolbar makes it easy to manage your messages on the move, with direct access to the most common functions, including reply and forward. If you have an AirPrint compatible printer you can also print messages over your wireless network.

your battery more quickly. Of course, if you're waiting for an urgent message you can still check manually from the Mail application by dragging down the message list so that the most recent entry pulls away from the top of the screen (see the grab, on the previous spread). Once you've picked up your messages, you will naturally sort through them, reading them, replying to

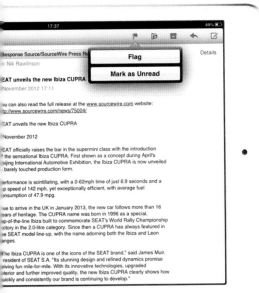

the ones that need immediate action, and postponing others. A lot of messages can be deleted right away, which you can do by tapping the Bin icon at the top of the screen, at which point the message will sweep up into the trash. See the box to the left for a quicker way to delete multiple messages if you're doing an initial scan on the move and don't want to read every message.

Others messages will need some thought, and so naturally you will want to mark them as unread or flag them for following up. To do this, and with the email open on your iPad mini screen, tap the flag on the upper toolbar and select Mark as Unread (see grab, left).

Sending messages

You can send a message from anywhere in the Mail application without having to return to the main mailbox screen, by tapping the small square and pencil icon in the top right-hand corner.

If you already know the address of the person you want to message you can type it straight in and Mail will attempt to complete the name that you're typing on the basis of previous messages and stored Contacts, but it is often easier to tap the blue '+' icon to the right of the To field and select the person from your contacts list where you'll be given the chance to pick the appropriate address if they have more than one on their record.

The procedure for replying to messages that you are reading is the same as above, except that instead of tapping the square and pencil icon, you tap on the backwards-pointing arrow, which would give you the option of either forwarding or replying to the presently-displayed message (see above)

Tip: Remote images

It's worth spending some time working your way through the various Mail options in the Settings app.

Among the most useful is the option to turn off the downloading of remote images in HTML messages (see grab, below). If you have a cell-enabled iPad mini doing this will save you from using up more of your monthly bandwidth allocation than you need, but even if you only have a Wi-Fi device it's also worth considering turning this off.

Downloading remote images, which may be uniquely tagged, can confirm that your address is active, and therefore could attract increased levels of spam in the future.

VIP mailbox

New in iOS 6 is the VIP mailbox, which lets you specify which if your contacts are of higher priority than the others so that you can get to their messages without wading through a deluge of other incoming emails. You can think of it in a similar manner to the Priority Inbox that Google introduced to Gmail a couple of years ago, although without the automated working out of what is most important.

Setting up the VIP mailbox is quite simple, and is something that you'll do bit by bit over time.

When you first start using your iPad mini, the VIP mailbox will be empty. However, the first time you receive a message from an important contact, tap their name on the From line of the message display and then tap Add to VIP. Immediately, their email address will have a star added to it, and you'll notice that similar stars appear beside each of the other messages you

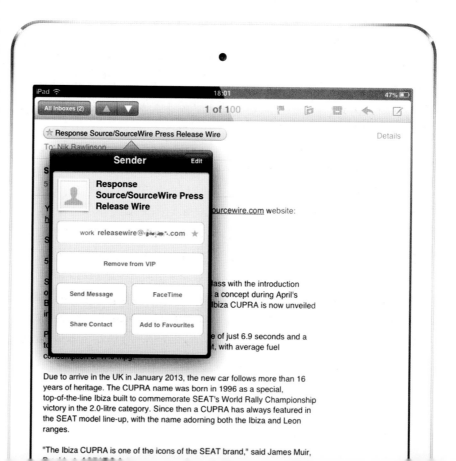

Due to arrive in the UK in January 2013, the new car follows more than 16 years of heritage. The CUPRA name was born in 1996 as a special, top-of-the-line Ibiza built to commemorate SEAT's World Rally Championship victory in the 2.0-litre category. Since then a CUPRA has always featured in the SEAT model line-up, with the name adorning both the Ibiza and Leon ranges.

"The Ibiza CUPRA is one of the icons of the SEAT brand," said James Muir,

Dedicated VIP settings let you change the way more important incoming messages are notified

have received from them that still reside in your inbox.

After adding contacts to your VIP list you can use the VIP settings in the centralised Settings app to change the way that notifications handle the arrival of email from these contacts (tap Settings | Notifications | VIP). Here, you can optionally setting a different email notification tone so you know you don't need to hurry to check your mail if you hear anything else.

Note that the VIP settings won't appear in the Settings app if you haven't conferred VIP status on any addresses yet.

Quick tip: Setting an email signature

You should set a signature to appear at the foot of every email. This is the digital equivalent of headed note paper, giving you an opportunity to promote your website or, in the case of many businesses, to position a legal disclaimer.

To do this tap Settings | Mail, Contacts, Calendars | Signature (below) and choose whether you want one single signature for all accounts, or a separate one for each. It is good practice to precede your signature with two dashes and a space ('-- ') and then start the footer on the next line down. In this way, most email clients will trim it off when your message is quoted back to you in a subsequent email and both save on bandwidth use and prevent your details being passed on.

Managing defaults

Several core iPad mini features, such as emailing links from Safari or jottings from the Notes app, will always use your default email address to dispatch messages. The default address is whichever one you set up first. If you've set up several accounts and would like one of your later additions to work as the default, and so handle email from other iPad mini applications, change it through Settings | Mail, Contacts, Calendars | Default Account.

Safari

Your window on the web

Safari is the iPad mini's web browser. By default it's found on the Dock so that it appears on every home screen – that's how important it is. As with a Mac or PC, you can swap it out for an alternative, such as the excellent Chrome from Google, but you can't ever make an alternative browser your default option for web work. That means that any links you open from emails or other applications will always be sent to Safari.

If you use Safari on the Mac or PC, many of its controls and interface elements will already look familiar. The toolbar that runs across the top of the screen has your forward and back controls, a button for opening new browser windows, the bookmark manager (it looks like an open book) and the shortcut saver and sharer (the box with an arrow). At the top of the screen are two input boxes: one for the web addresses you want to visit and the other for entering search terms that you want to send to Google. To date, Apple hasn't adopted a unified search and address bar here the way it has on the Mac, which does away with the stand-alone search box.

When you first fire up Safari, it's set to use Google for its search results. It references the main .com version of the site, and

Although you can't select a localised version of any of the search engines on offer, you can switch between Google (the default), Yahoo! and Bing.

although you can't change this to a localised national version you can switch away from Google wholesale if you choose, picking from either Yahoo! or Bing as alternatives by tapping Settings | Safari | Search Engine.

In common with many other iPad mini applications, and the version of Safari that ships with OS X, this mobile edition does an excellent job of recognising the dimensions of both your page and the elements positioned on it. Turn it to portrait or landscape orientation and you'll see that it resizes the content to fit the width of the screen, allowing you to choose between a wider, larger display, or a taller view that shows you more of each page. It also knows the dimensions of everything on the page so that double-tapping any element, such as a column of text, zooms the content until that element takes up the whole width of the screen, whichever way up you have it. You can now perform the same trick on the desktop by double-tapping a trackpad on any Mac running Safari 5 or later.

Reading view

Good though Safari's automatic resizing of content is when you double-tap, there are times when you simply don't need all of the content on a page that's surrounding what you're trying to read. Neither do you need the adverts and banners that appear within the page.

At times like this you can strip them out by switching to the Reader view, which isolates the main body content and presents just that, free of ads and distractions. Rather cleverly, it also recognises when a story spreads itself across several pages and stitches them all together so that you can scroll straight through the content without having to click from one page to another.

The Reader view is invoked by tapping the button marked 'Reader' next to the page address in the URL bar. When you've finished reading, tapping Done returns you to the original page. Meanwhile, dedicated controls in the Reader view let you change the font size and share the stripped-out content by email, over social networks and so on.

Emailing a web page's contents in this way is a more efficient way to bring it to your contacts' attention as the Reader view sends the content of the page in the body of the email, complete with a link back to the source and a selection of styled fonts and embedded graphics. Be careful when emailing content from someone else's website to observe any usage restrictions, including copyright.

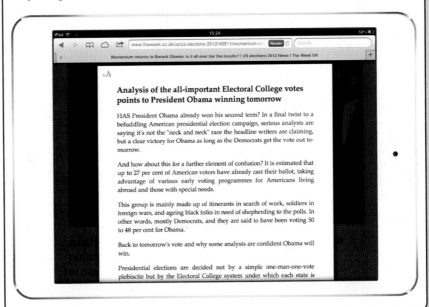

How to: Search in Safari

All of Safari's controls are clustered on the toolbar that runs across the top of the screen, with many of the buttons sporting pop-up dialogues that reveal hidden features.

Tap on the address box and start typing in the URL of the page you want, and a list of matching addresses you have recently visited will drop down so you can pick the one you want without typing the whole address. Likewise, start typing in the search box and it will drop down a list of suggestions from Google or your chosen alternative if you've set one through Settings and, below the list, any searches you have recently performed that match what you have typed over your last few browsing sessions.

The search box also intelligently searches the page you're currently browsing. Simply type in the term you want to find on the page, and the search results will show you how many times it appears on the current page. Scroll up the list of results until you reach the very bottom entry and tap the search term under the 'On This Page' bar (see below left).

This switches you back to your page and highlights the first match for your search term in yellow (see below right). Using the left and right arrows to the left of the toolbar steps you backwards and forwards through the remaining matches, with a counter to the right showing which match you're currently viewing.

Stepping forwards or backwards beyond the last or first match loops the page so that you return to the next hit at the start or end of the list. You can also use the search box on this bar directly to change the term that you're searching for on the current page.

How to: Add bookmarks to the iPad mini home screen

While it isn't exactly difficult to find your favourite pages in a regular list of bookmarks, it makes sense to save your most-used links to your iPad mini Home screen, at which point they will launch like applications, without the Safari location toolbar in view and feel much more like a dedicated app.

[1] Navigate to the page you want to link to and tap the shortcut button on the toolbar. This brings up the standard list of Safari controls, many of which – such as Twitter, Message, Mail and Facebook – are shared with other apps. Tap Add to Home Screen (see below left) to save the link as a with an icon.

[2] If the site doesn't have its own dedicated icon, Safari will create one using a thumbnail from the web page itself. Developers can create their own, and your iPad mini will respect this and use it in place

on the home screen if it exists. All you need to do is give it a name that will make it easy to recognise among your applications (below right).

[3] Your link will be added to your home screen and to all intents and purposes acts just like any regular application link, which means that if you find you are using it frequently you can drag it to the Dock.

[4] To remove a link from the Home screen, hold your finger on it until the icons start to shiver and each sprouts a small 'x' in a circle. Tap this and then confirm that you want to delete the bookmark.

Be careful when removing saved links in this way as no backup is stored in your regular bookmark list. If you want to set one, first tap the link to open it, save the bookmark and only then delete the icon.

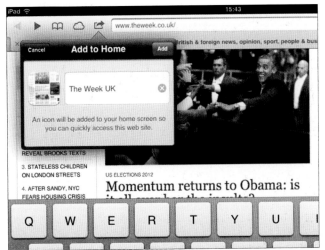

iCloud tabs

Although it can perform other functions, like help you find a lost iPad mini, iCloud is primarily focused on one thing: synchronisation. It's not surprising, then, to see Apple introduce the concept of iCloud tabs in iOS 6 and OS X 10.8 Mountain Lion.

Quite simply, iCloud tabs synchronise your open pages between your various devices, so that if you were reading an online report on your Mac before leaving work it would be ready for you to carry on reading on your iPad mini or iPhone during your commute home. You wouldn't need to email a link to yourself or save it as a bookmark on any of your devices for this to work. In iOS, anything open on another iOS device, or a Mac, appears in the list under iCloud tabs. On the Mac, open tabs on other devices are displayed on a drop-down dialogue box.

If you have all the necessary kit and are updated to the latest versions of iOS, OS X and Safari,

and still find that iCloud tabs isn't working for you, check that it's enabled on each of your devices. On the Mac, open System Preferences | iCloud and check that Bookmark syncing is active. On your iPad mini, go to Settings

| iCloud and check that the slider beside Safari is set to ON.

Sadly, iCloud tabs is a Mac-only feature as Apple didn't ship a version of Safari 6 for Windows when it released the OS X edition.

How to use: Safari Reading List

Reading List was introduced in iOS 5, alongside an equivalent feature on Mac OS X Lion. It was improved in iOS 6 and OS X 10.8 Mountain Lion.

Recognising that we all have far busier lifestyles now, Apple has implemented this tool, which allows us to keep a note of pages we want to come back to when we have more time on any iOS or OS X device running those operating systems.

To mark a page in your Reading List, click the action button on the toolbar below your browser window (the curved arrow leaping out of a box) and select Add to Reading List. The page will be stored in the Reading List section of the regular Safari bookmarks (see right). Tapping the Reading List entry opens up the list of links you have already saved.

The same feature appears in Safari on the Mac and PC (above right), where a pair of glasses on the Bookmarks toolbar lets you save a page in the sidebar.

If you've signed up for a free iCloud account you can set it to synchronise your Reading List entries automatically, so that whichever device you are using when you have some free time to catch up on what you've missed, the List will be waiting.

The really smart part of Reading List is that in the latest update it not only keeps track of the pages you have marked, but downloads their contents, too, so that even if you don't have network coverage – perhaps because you're in an area with poor propagation, or you're on a flight with your iPad mini in Airplane Mode – you can still read the content of the saved pages from the Safari cache.

Twitter
Microblogging from your iPad mini

Twitter, the web-based messaging system that has taken the world by storm, is now a core feature of iOS on the iPhone, iPad and iPad mini. It has been built in at the heart of the operating system since the release of iOS 5, which makes it easier than ever to send short links and notes to your friends directly from inside some of the most important pre-installed applications.

Although you'll enjoy the best Twitter experience if you download a full-featured client, you can actually tweet without the client from Notification Centre, where you'll also see your replies coming in, and of course use the Twitter website, which works flawlessly through the default iOS browser, Safari.

It is so closely integrated with the main features of iOS that it's set up directly in the default Settings app. Here we'll look at how you can add your Twitter account to your iPad mini and send your first direct tweet.

How to: Sign up to Twitter and send your first tweet

01 Tap Settings | Twitter to open the Twitter settings pane and then start the process by tapping Add Account and entering your credentials. You can't actually sign up to Twitter through the Settings app, so if you don't already have an account of your own point a regular browser at twitter.com and join there. Accounts are free.

02 Allow your iPad mini to add Twitter contacts to the records in your address book. It does this by comparing your contacts' details with records already assigned to Twitter accounts and adding the Twitter usernames to any matching cards that it finds. It makes sense to repeat this process periodically to keep everything up to date.

Twitter works well in Safari, the iPad mini's default browser. However, if you prefer to use a dedicated app then you can download a free Twitter client from the App Store. You can also tweet directly from various applications within iOS 6 by using the sharing shortcut, as we'll show you over the following pages.

03 To send a message to a contact on Twitter, open the Contacts application and find their card. If they have signed up to Twitter then their username should appear in the dedicated Twitter box without you having entered it yourself, as it was drawn down in step 02. Tap this, followed by Tweet to send them a message.

04 Your message is sent as a mention so will also be visible to anyone else who follows both you and them. To make it private, replace the leading @ with a D followed by a space. You can optionally add your location, which is drawn from the iPad mini's Location Services, by tapping Add Location. Keep an eye on the message length countdown.

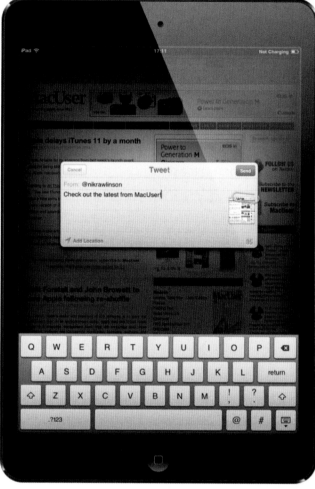

Tweeting from apps Several of the native iOS applications let you send tweets directly from their share menus. These work in much the same way as the Share Sheets that Apple debuted in OS X 10.8.

The range of choices open to you when it comes to sharing data will be tailored on a per-app basis, with some offering more options than others, but in general Twitter is well supported.

Many sport an action button, which looks like an arrow coming out of a box, which opens up your sharing options, but others, such as maps (see right) have a dedicated sharing button stowed away on a secondary page.

Tweeting from Safari Twitter is a great way to share links with family and friends, and a well populated Twitter stream with links relevant to a single subject can often attract a strong following from others who have an interest in that field. To tweet directly from Safari visit the page that you want to publicise and then tap the shortcut button on the toolbar. This picks up the regular menu for adding bookmarks or saving a link to the file to your reading list, which in iOS 5 now also includes an option to tweet. All you need do is write a short covering note to explain to your followers what the linked page is about and your iPad mini will send it straight to your followers.

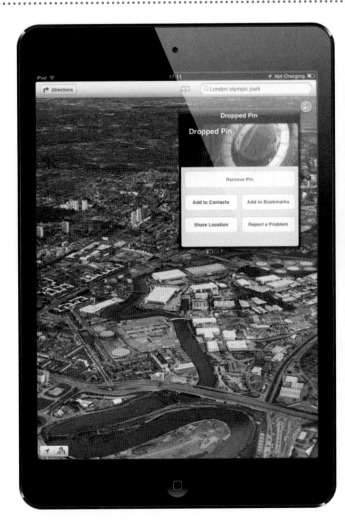

Tweeting from Maps Twitter is a great way to organise a meeting with your friends. If you want to do so on an ad-hoc basis then you can use the iOS Maps application to tweet suggested locations to your friends.

Start by locating your chosen spot on the map by using the regular search tools. Maps will drop a marker on the map identifying the destination, on the end of which you'll see an arrow in a blue circle.

Tap the arrow to switch to the information pane (see above) and then tap Share Location. You'll see the regular choice of sharing methods, so tap Twitter and the location will be tagged to a new message.

Tweeting from alternative accounts iOS allows you to sign in to more than one Twitter account at a time and switch between them depending on what you want to post. This lets you separate your subjects according to the interests of your followers with, say, gardening tweets going to one group and your general thoughts and opinions to another.

To change between the two accounts, follow whichever method is relevant to the content you want to post, and when the tweeting interface is displayed tap on the username of whichever account is currently active. This will call up a dialogue with each of the accounts you've set up (see above).

Facebook
Posting from your iPad mini

Facebook has finally joined Twitter as the second social network in iOS, appearing one release behind Twitter in iOS 6.

Signing in through the iOS Settings app works in much the same way as signing in to Twitter, and it allows you to share content with your Facebook friends directly from both native and third-party iOS applications, and the Twitter app itself.

Once again, just like when you sign up with Twitter, it offers to update your contacts by adding their Facebook account details and photos to your iPad mini Contacts book. Those that have been added will have a Facebook 'f' stamped on their avatars (see grab, right).

Enabling your Facebook account on iOS also allows it to add your Facebook events to your calendar and keep them updated, and activates the post to Facebook button on the sharing shortcut in various iOS applications. Over time, as

How to: Post to Facebook using iOS 6

01 The easiest way to send a quick update to Facebook without opening a Facebook client is to pull down on the clock to open Notification Center and then tap in the Tap to Post box on the right of the top line. Note that it sits beside the Twitter box, so don't get them mixed up or you'll address the wrong set of friends.

02 However, you can also post content direct from other applications installed on your iPad mini. Here we are using the Photos application and have tapped the share button on the upper toolbar. This calls up the various ways in which you can share your content with friends, on the second line of which is the Facebook option. Tap this.

A Facebook badge on this Contacts icon indicates that it includes data drawn down from the popular social network

you add new applications from the App Store, they will also be able to use your Facebook login details if you specifically grant them access. Only do this if you understand what rights they will have to post to your wall and what access they will have to your friends' data and contact information.

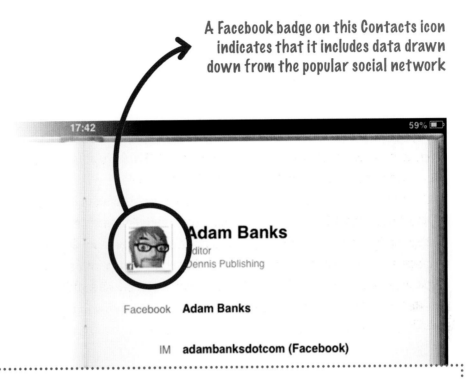

03 This calls up the Facebook posting card with the photo that we want to post to our account clipped to it. Here we are writing a short description so that it makes sense when it appears on our account, as it's not immediately obvious what the image depicts. We can geo-locate it by tapping the Add Location link below it and tap Post to send it.

04 Facebook lets you organise your contacts into groups, and you can make your post visible to just a small selection by tapping Friends in the lower right corner of the card and selecting a group. These categories are set in your Facebook account, so if you want to change them you'll have to log in through the browser at *facebook.com*.

Messages

Send texts, photos, files and more... for free

Messages is Apple's proprietary messaging system, designed to be used as a supplement to regular text and picture messaging on devices running iOS 5 and later. In effect, it adds a kind of text messaging feature to the iPad, iPad mini and iPod touch, none of which had that feature before.

Before you can use it, you must enable the underlying iMessage service by opening Settings | Messages, and tapping the OFF/ON switch beside iMessage to activate the service (see below). You then need to

decide how people can contact you, selecting from registered addresses and iPhone numbers.

By default, Messages is set up to use your Apple ID, but if it's not also your primary email address there's a fair chance that people won't know it and so won't be able to get hold of you that way. Remedy this by adding further contact details by tapping Send & Receive and adding email addresses and the numbers of any iPhones that you own, which are running iOS 5 or later, to the list of available options.

Scroll down to the Send & Receive box and tap it, then start

by tapping Add Another Email... and enter the address with which it will be easiest for your contacts to find you on the Messages system.

Each time you add a new address, Messages will verify that it is valid and, if it is, it'll put a tick to the left of it in the table.

If you want to remove an address, either now or at some point in the future, tap the blue chevron at the far right of its line

You can skip Messages set-up if you added your contact details when initialising your iPad mini using the screen below.

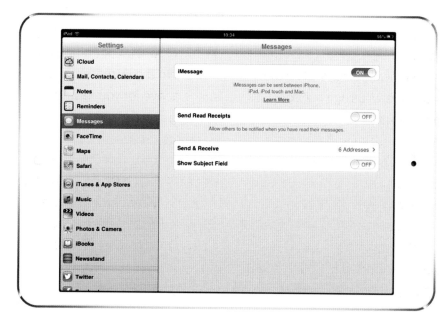

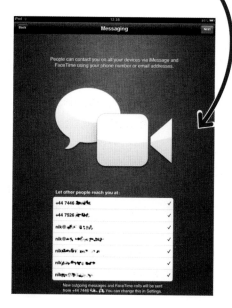

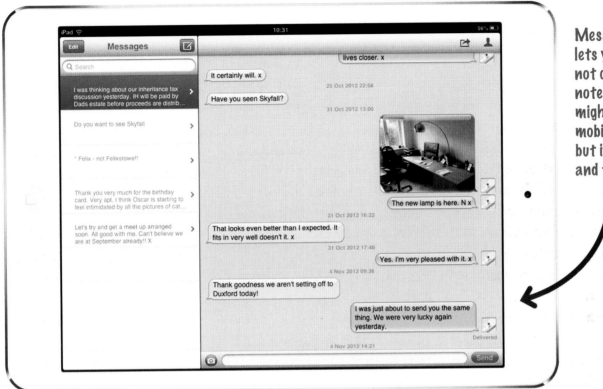

Messages lets you share not only text notes, as you might on a mobile phone, but images and files, too.

on the table and select Remove This Email.

If you have an iPhone you can only add its number to your list of authorised reception points for Messages from the phone itself, so repeat this process there and it will show up on your iPad mini.

If you add several contact options in this way you might find that Messages sets one of your least-used addresses as the default originator of new conversations. You can change this quite simply by scrolling further down the screen and picking an alternative in the Start new conversations from: panel.

When you've finished setting it up, you can exit the Messages preferences and start using the app itself.

You can send messages directly by tapping on the Messages app on the home screen and typing in what you want to say, using your contact's email address or their phone number as the destination, or picking someone from your Contacts list. Some core apps in iOS 6 and iOS 5 also hook into Messages as a conduit through which to send their contents from the sharing tab that appears when you tap a toolbar icon.

For example, open an image from the Photos app and tap the shortcut button on the top toolbar (the curved arrow coming out of a rectangular box). Here you'll find an option for Message which, when tapped, drops your image into a new message with space above for you to write a covering note.

Messages synchronise through iCloud so if you have several iOS devices you'll find the same stream on each of them. They also appear in the Mac, although for Windows users there's no way to access the Messages stream on a PC.

FaceTime
Video conferencing for free

FaceTime is Apple's rapidly maturing video conferencing tool. It appeared in iOS 4 and has since reached out onto OS X, the company's operating system for its Mac line of computers.

This extension of the platform allows users with an iPad mini, iPad, iPhone, iPod touch or Mac (with suitable camera if they aren't using a portable Mac or iMac, which has the renamed FaceTime camera built in to the lid or the bezel of the screen) to talk to each other by video, in real time, without paying any call charges.

How to use FaceTime

FaceTime uses the Internet to patch together the users at either end of the connection. Because of the amount of data that it needs to pass between the two participants to maintain a constant, smooth video stream, it took until the arrival of iOS 6 for it to be possible to make FaceTime calls over the 3G or 4G cellphone network. Note that

doing so could have a serious impact on the amount of data you still have available to use from your monthly allowance for other browsing activities if you use FaceTime in this way on a regular basis.

To place a FaceTime call you need to have an Apple ID. If you are signed up to iCloud then you can use your login details for that service to access FaceTime. However, if you don't you can get yourself a free ID at *https://appleid.apple.com/* or by signing up through the FaceTime preferences in the Settings app.

Setting up FaceTime

01 FaceTime may be switched off on your iPad mini, so the first thing you need to do is check that it's active. Open its preferences by launching the Settings app and tapping FaceTime. Check that the slider beside FaceTime is set to ON. If it isn't, tap it to wake it up. (see grab, above)

02 At this point FaceTime will probably be set to only send incoming calls to your iPad mini by way of your Apple ID, which as we explained in relation to Messages might not be something that your contacts know. You should therefore add some extra contact points.

Tap Add Another Email... and enter the address you want to use. Once again, as with Messages, FaceTime will verify that the address is valid and, if it is, will drop a tick beside it in the left hand column. If you want to remove an address simply tap the chevron to the right, followed by Remove This Email.

If you want to add a phone number currently assigned to an iPhone to the list of contact points through which people can reach you on FaceTime you'll have to do this directly on the iPhone itself.

03 To make your own outgoing FaceTime call, tap the FaceTime application (if you have an iPhone you'll already know that the appearance of a dedicated FaceTime application is a point of difference with the iPad mini (and iPad), as on the iPhone you make FaceTime calls through the regular Phone application). If you prefer, you can alternatively start a FaceTime call by tapping the FaceTime button against a contact's details in your iOS address book.

Scroll down the list of names that appear on the right of the FaceTime screen (see grab, left) until you find the one you want to talk to and tap it. The front-mounted camera will become active and your iPad mini will initiate the call over your wireless network. Assuming it's successful, your image will shrink to a small thumbnail in the corner of the screen so that you can see the other person's image more clearly. If you want to show them a view of what you can see in front of you, tap the spin button to switch to the rear camera.

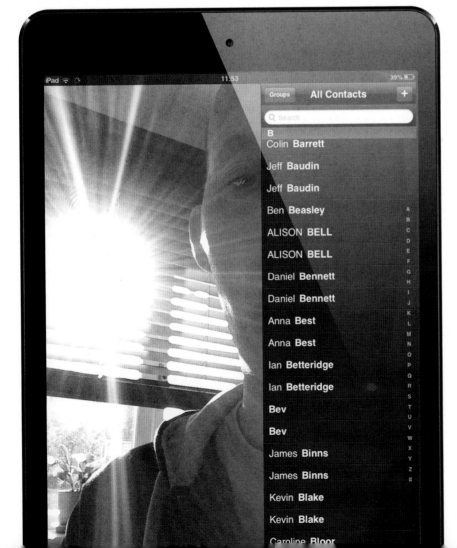

Find Friends

Easily locate the people who matter the most

Find My Friends is Apple's own people-locating application. It works on the iPad mini, iPad and iPhone, and uses data from the cellphone network or Wi-Fi connection to plot another user on your device, allowing you to quickly and easily find where they are. It isn't installed by default, but it's a free download from the App Store (search for Find My Friends). Once you've downloaded it, log in using your regular Apple ID credentials.

Clearly Apple couldn't put out this kind of tracking information without first gaining users'

permission, so your first step is to send a message to your friends and ask them to allow you to see their location. They'll need an iOS device of their own for this to work.

Turn your iPad to landscape orientation and tap the '+' button at the top of the sidebar. Enter the name of the friend you want to find and, optionally, add a message of your own – particularly if you think they might not know what Find My Friends is all about (see below).

Apple will send them an email containing a link (bottom of the opposite page) which when

Privacy

In the same way that you can track your friends' movements, they can track yours.

You can authorise a temporary pass for them to see where you are if they're trying to direct you to a destination, but if you've given them full access and need to revoke it at some point in the future you can do so by tapping Me on the toolbar, selecting the follower and tapping Remove from Followers.

You can also de-authorise Find My Friends altogether by turning off its access to Location Services. Do this by opening the Settings app and tapping Privacy | Location Services and tapping the ON/OFF slider beside Find Friends.

You can track several people at once using Find My Friends, which makes it easy to direct each one of them to the location of a group meeting.

tapped on an iOS device takes them to their own copy of Find My Friends so that they can accept or refuse your request.

Each of your authorised friends will now appear in the Find My Friends sidebar, from where you can tap between them to view each person's location on a map in either plan, satellite or hybrid view. A small badge beside their name shows how far they are from your current location (see above), with a

floating flag pinpointing their position.

At the bottom of the screen you'll see their current address (this may be an approximation rather than a specific door number and street name) and options to open their full contact information and directions from your position to theirs.

This final option drops you out of Find My Friends and into the Maps application, which plots the quickest routes by private vehicle, public transport or foot in the usual manner (see right).

Find My Friends can also work in reverse, with you temporarily allowing contacts to see your location. This is particularly useful if, say, you're attending a trade show and your colleagues need

to be able to find you at short notice. In this situation, tap the Temporary button on the toolbar at the foot of the interface and enter the contact details to which the invitation to see your location should be sent, along with an expiry date after which they won't be able to track you any longer.

Bear in mind that activating Location Services in this way can run down your battery more quickly than usual.

App Store
The easy way to extend your iPad mini's abilities

For many people, the biggest problem with the original iPhone, the ultimate great grandparent of the iPad mini, was the fact it was a closed, sealed unit. And we're not just talking about the hardware, for just as you couldn't change or upgrade the battery or memory, you also couldn't install your own applications either. Well, not legally, anyway.

In truth some enterprising coders found workarounds that allowed them to hack a way into the iPhone's operating system and add their own applications to its core system files – or those they had downloaded from the net. It worked, but it was risky, as Apple didn't authorise such modifications. This meant that some users who had hacked their iPhone discovered that it no longer worked after downloading a firmware update.

Known as Jailbreaking, this practice continues, on iPads as well as iPhones, with many users now Jailbreaking their old, out-of-warranty devices that can no longer receive updates to iOS, or more recent devices on which they want to install applications that haven't been authorised for sale through the App Store.

Apps go official

Recognising that apps were a fertile market from which it could profit, Apple soon announced a Software Development Kit, and a store through which developers could sell their work. It's not surprising, then, that by the time he stepped on stage to announce the iPhone 3G, around a half of Steve Jobs' script concerned itself with the new applications that had been written specifically for the iPhone by third-party developers and Apple itself.

When Phil Schiller stepped on stage to announce the iPad mini, he reinforced the fact that several hundred thousand apps have now been written specifically for the iPad, rather than simply being upsized from the iPhone, making this one of the most exciting tablet devices you can buy.

Every application on the App Store, which is accessed through iTunes on your Mac or PC, or the App Store application on your iPad mini, must be approved by Apple. This might sound draconian, but it ensures that

What about a refund?

All purchases through the App Store are considered final, so make sure that you really do want a particular application before tapping the button to buy it, unless it's a free app. If there is a problem with the application (which is unlikely as all apps are checked by Apple before they are made available on the Store) then you may be able to apply for a refund. However, there is no opportunity to ask for a refund simply because a product is reduced in price after you have bought it, and both in-app purchases and subscriptions are also considered to be final purchases, so keep an eye on when a subscription is due to be renewed and make sure that you cancel it in good time if you don't want to continue when your current subscription expires.

everything you install on your device is safe, and should run without any problems.

They can be free or charged-for, and all are developed using Apple's free Software Development Kit. Before they can have their applications certified for use on the iPhone, however, developers must pay a $99 registration fee that buys them an electronic certificate to prove to Apple who they are, and that they are a reliable developer.

Large applications must be downloaded through iTunes on your Mac or PC or by Wi-Fi, but applications of 10MB or less, can be downloaded wirelessly over the mobile phone network direct to the iPad mini itself if you have one that includes

cell connectivity. Each one is registered on the iPad mini, which monitors the App Store for updates and notifies you of any that have updated editions available for download by posting a small red number beside the App Store icon.

For developers, Jobs outlined six key benefits in developing for the iPhone and distributing applications through the App Store. Key among these was the fact that the developer gets to keep 70% of revenues, and that they themselves can pick

Your iPad mini keeps track of which apps you have already installed through the App Store and notifies you of any recently-posted updates by overlaying the App Store icon with a badge showing how many new free downloads are waiting for you to grab them.

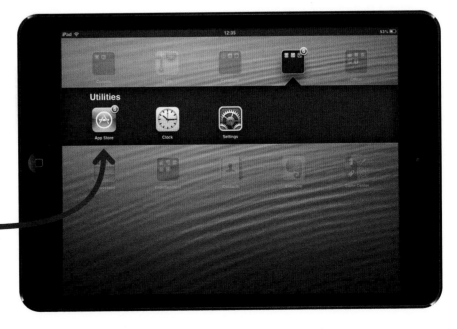

Synchronisation quick tip

Turn on synchronisation in the iCloud preferences pane to have your iPad mini download books, music and applications that you buy on other devices, including iTunes on your Mac or PC.

the price at which they sell their products – so long as they match specific price-points set by Apple. Apart from the wide range of free applications on the Store, the cheapest software costs just 79p (in the UK) or 99c (in the US and Europe) to download.

Other benefits include access to Apple's payment mechanism, meaning that developers don't have to deal with credit card payments themselves (which is also a benefit for us end-users as it means we are always dealing with a trusted company – Apple), no hosting costs, no marketing fees and, perhaps most important of all, regular payments.

More impressive, from a developer's point of view, is that as the applications are hosted within the iTunes Store, they benefit from Apple's own digital rights management software,

FairPlay, so end-users won't be able to buy a single copy and then pass them around between one another.

If you would like to try your own hand at developing applications for the iPad mini, the software development kit can be downloaded from *developer. apple.com/programs/ios*.

App Store applications

So what can you expect to find on the App Store? The complete catalogue runs the full gamut, all the way from games to business applications.

Games play a key part, with Apple now boasting one of the strongest mobile gaming platforms in the world, but the iPad mini is equally well catered for in the business world, with complete office suites, financial applications, expense managers

and more lining up to serve the world of commerce.

Fans of social networking will welcome the many tools for uploading images direct to Flickr, chatting with friends on Twitter, updating your Facebook status and posting to friends' Walls. You might wonder why you'd want either of these two latter applications when iOS 6 has both Twitter and Facebook built in, but in truth they're key to gaining a fully-features experience on either social network without resorting to the browser.

If you'd rather not rely on trawling the web yourself or using an online RSS reader then check out one of the RSS apps, or indeed the dedicated newspaper and magazine applications from some of the UK's biggest broadsheet and tabloid publishers. For your fortnightly fix of Mac and iPad news, be sure to search for MacUser's application, which presents a digital copy of every issue for viewing on an iPad, iPad mini or iPhone screen.

All can be reviewed and rated so you can see what others

thought of each one before you spend any money, but do bear in mind that most often those who give ratings to anything from a holiday to a service to an app are those who have not enjoyed the experience rather than those who have. How often do we feel more motivated to complain rather than complement, after all? Far less than when we've had a bad experience, in almost every instance. It's therefore worth reading a few reviews rather than stopping after the first bad one.

Use the search tools to find applications on the basis of name or function, or use the Genius function to have the App Store make recommendations of applications that you will find useful or entertaining based on your previous buying patterns.

Signing up for downloads

Before you can download anything from an Apple Store, of which the App Store is a part, just like the iTunes Store, you need to sign up for an Apple ID.

If you have downloaded music from the Store for use on an iPod then you already have an ID – just as you have if you are an iCloud or former MobileMe or .Mac subscriber. If not, then the easiest way to get yourself an Apple ID is within the iPad mini itself. Tap Settings | Mail, Contacts, Calendars | Add Account... | iCloud | Get Free Apple ID.

Buying applications directly through iOS

Although you can download applications using iTunes on your Mac or PC, it's even easier to download through your iPad mini.

Apple maintains extensive lists of the best-selling paid-for apps and most popular free applications, but the smartest way to find what you're looking for is to search directly.

Use the search box at the top of the screen to enter a keyword, subject, app name or publisher. Here we have searched for Dennis Publishing, which has an extensive list of dedicated magazine apps.

The results of your search are presented in a series of panels (see above). Swipe through them until you find the one you're after – in this case, MacUser – and then tap the button to directly install it on your iPad mini. If it's a charged-for application, the price will be displayed below the application name.

If you're unsure whether or not you've found the app you're after, tap the application icon at the top of the panel to open further details, including screen grabs, reviews from other users and a list of related applications that might also interest you.

iCloud
Your files, photos and data online

When Apple retired MobileMe, it's long-running but not particularly loved online service, it replaced it in autumn 2011 with the subtly different iCloud. MobileMe's old freeform iDisk didn't survive the move, and neither did the galleries feature (although you can now create Journals using iPhoto and, as we'll show over the page, you can share your images using a Shared Photo Stream).

However, iCloud does still have a full set of tools for managing your email, organising your contacts and maintaining your calendar. These each synchronise their contents with the Mail, Contacts and Calendar applications on the iPad mini, and have matching online applications that you can access by logging in with your regular Apple ID at *icloud.com*.

As well as synchronising your day-to-day appointments and

contacts, iCloud can be used to maintain a backup of your iPad mini's contents so that should the unthinkable happen and you lose your device you'll at least not lose all of your data at the same time, and it can be used to share documents with a Mac courtesy of Documents in the Cloud, which works brilliantly with Apple's own office suite, iWork, and is now being integrated into a host of third-party applications for use on iOS and the Mac.

Signing up for an iCloud account

iCloud accounts are free, but you do need to have an iPad mini, iPad, iPhone or iPod touch running iOS 5 or later, or a Mac running OS X 10.7 Lion or later.

To sign up on your iPad mini, open the Settings application and tap Mail, Contacts, Calendars | Add Account... | iCloud | Get a Free Apple ID. If you already have an account with the App Store then your Apple ID is the details you use to log in here.

How to: Manage your iCloud storage

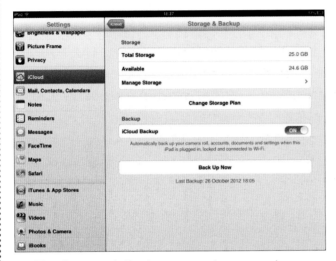

01 The Storage & Backup page shows you how much space you're using. We've used less than 1GB. Tap Manage Storage to see what's eating up the available space on your account.

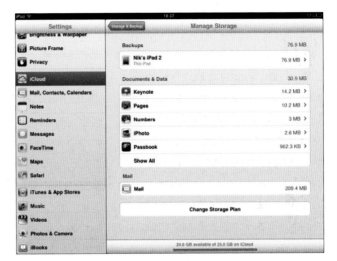

02 One of our apps, Pages, is using 8.6MB of storage on our account. As Pages is stored locally on our iPad mini we know that this is purely consumed by docs. Tap Pages to see which ones.

03 The largest file in our iCloud account is almost 900KB. That's not a great deal of space, but as we're not using it any more we may as well remove it by tapping Edit and then using the bars left of each file to bring up their dedicated Delete buttons.

04 If you can't delete any of your files but still need more room to work with, return to the Storage & Backup page and tap Change Storage Plan. Apple gives you the choice of either 20GB or 50GB of additional space. You choose.

Photo Stream

iCloud can store up to 1000 of your most recent images in what it calls a Photo Stream. These images can be taken on any iOS device and, because they're stored on Apple's servers as well as your local iDevice, they're available to all other iOS devices logged in to your iCloud account. This way, the photo you took on you iPhone could be inserted into a Keynote slide that you're designing on your iPad mini.

How to: Sync your photos to Photo Stream

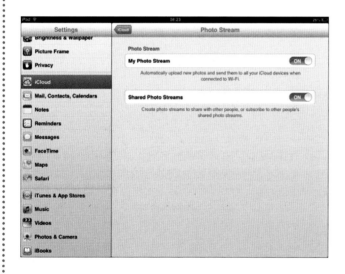

01 Make sure the iCloud Photo Stream is enabled by tapping Settings > iCloud > Photo Stream and tapping the ON/OFF slider so that it shows ON.

You'll notice that there's also an option here to enable Shared Photo Streams. This is a new feature in iOS 6, which allows you to make your photos public or share them with specific invited contacts. You can create several Shared Photo Streams that sit separately from your regular synchronised Photo Stream, and each one will be automatically updated as you add new images to it, so you don't need to manually re-publish everything.

02 Open the Pictures application, where you will see a Photo Stream button on the top toolbar. Tap this, followed by My Photo Stream, and if you have taken any photos on another iOS 5- or iOS 6-enabled device logged into an iCloud account with Photo Stream active they will automatically appear here. Images taken on your local iPad mini also appear here, of course, as it's from this location that they're synchronised to your other iOS devices. The space taken up by the images in your Photo Stream doesn't count against the 5GB free iCloud allowance.

Photo Stream quick tip

Don't confuse the iCloud Photo Stream with the PhotoStream service maintained by photo sharing site Flickr.com. The two are completely different services, and are therefore incompatible with one another.

Images are also stored on your Mac, if you have one, in an enabled iPhoto or Aperture application, and on a PC in a specified folder. This gives you the freedom to shoot as many photos as you want on your device, safe in the knowledge that even if you have to delete the oldest ones to make space for new images they will be safely backed up elsewhere and can be easily retrieved, so long as you have turned on your synced computer in the last 30 days.

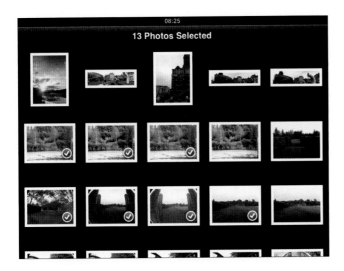

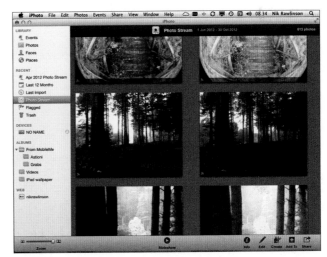

03 Images are automatically expired from your photo stream after 30 days, so if you spot something you like in your photo stream over that time that was taken using an alternative iOS device then you'll need to make sure you manually save it to your local photo store if you want to keep it. Tap the Edit button on the toolbar, then tap on each of the images you want to save. They will have a small blue tick overlaid on them to show that they are selected. If you tap one by mistake, tap it again to deselect it. When you have finished, tap Save and select a folder to which you want to save them.

04 The next time you fire up iPhoto or Aperture on your Mac while connected to the Internet it will download the contents of your Photo Stream and use it to update its own internal library – so long as you have enabled it in either application. On a Windows PC, the contents of your Photo Stream are stored in a regular folder, with a separate folder handling uploads. Unlike your live Photo Stream, iPhoto, Aperture and the folders in Windows don't retire images from the library after 30 days or 1000 shots so there's no need to manually duplicate them if you want to keep a copy.

Although you'll only have one primary synchronised Photo Stream sharing images between your iOS devices, you can set up multiple shared Streams for friends and family

How to: Share a Photo Stream

01 Start by selecting the images you want to work with, as you did when saving images to your Camera Roll, by tapping Edit and then tapping each one in turn. After that, tap the Share button and select Photo Stream as the method by which you want to share your images.

02 Enter the address of the contact with whom you want to share your Photo Stream, give the stream a name and choose whether it should be available to the public on an accessible site, then tap Next. Even if you do, the address won't be very easy to remember off the top of your head.

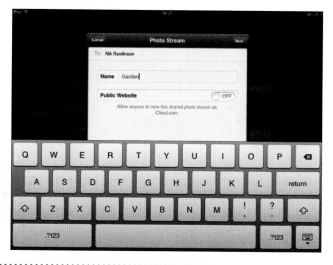

iCloud and Safari

If you use a Mac as well as an iPad mini and any other iOS devices, you can use iCloud to synchronise your browsing between your various installed editions of Safari using what Apple calls iCloud tabs. So long as it's enabled in the Settings app, iCloud tabs will feed back to the server whatever you are browsing on your iPad mini, iPad, iPhone or iPod touch running iOS 6 or later, and on a Mac running OS X 10.8 (Mountain Lion).

Direct links to each open page are displayed when you tap the cloud icon on the Safari toolbar on any of your devices so that you can quickly return to them. This would allow you to start reading something on your Mac at work, and finish reading it on your iPad mini on the train journey home without having to either email yourself a link or search for it anew.

Safari also now includes a reading pane to which you can

03 When your contact receives the invitation in their email inbox it will contain a direct link to your shared Photo Stream. To view your images they only need to click this and it will open in their browser, which is just as well, as the addresses are long strings of seemingly random characters.

04 If you later want to revoke either a public or shared Photo Stream, open the Photos app and tap the Photo Stream tab, followed by the Edit button. Now tap on the small circled cross on the top corner of the Photo Stream stack you want to delete. Tap Done when you have finished.

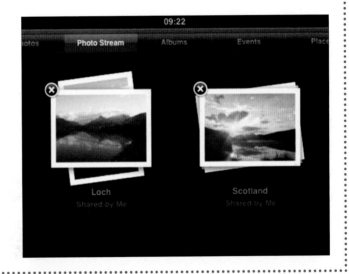

save links to pages that you don't have time to read right now, but want to pick up again at a later date. Again, these are synchronised over iCloud so that pages you save on your iPad mini are cached on a regular Mac and any other iOS devices that are logged in and synchronising to the same iCloud account.

Documents in the Cloud

One of the primary uses of cloud services, whichever provider they're from, is to synchronise your documents and data so that whichever device you're using, however you're connected and wherever you are, you can stay productive.

Documents in the Cloud affords this kind of flexibility to iPad mini users.

Having signed up to iCloud and enabled the Documents & Data option in the Settings application, this will automatically synchronise your work between the iPad mini and a Mac running OS X 10.8 or later.

Once up and running, all synchronisation is automatic and takes place in the background. However, while applications like Pages and Numbers automatically copy everything to the server (see right), some split their document management screens into areas, depending on the storage medium. You may therefore need to step back from internal storage to find iCloud.

How to: Synchronise your documents in iWork

The first time you use any of the iWork applications – Pages, Numbers or Keynote – on your iPad mini, they will ask if you want to use iCloud. If you want to synchronise your work across multiple devices, tap the option to allow it.

The main file management screen, which you can see below, contains floating individual documents represented by thumbnails and the folders into which you have organised them, represented by darker containers containing smaller

An arrow in the corner of a document icon indicates that it's queued for upload.

Progress bars track downloads so you know when they're complete.

The status line shows you how much more your iPad mini still has to transfer.

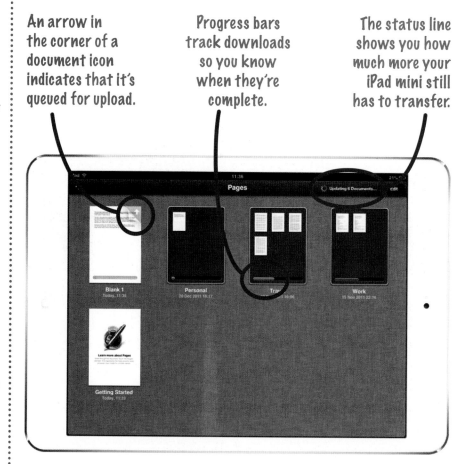

Bad news for Windows users: Apple doesn't yet produce versions of Pages, Numbers or Keynote for the PC, and hasn't hinted that there's any in the works, either, so you can't synchronise your documents back to your machine over iCloud.

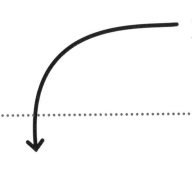

thumbnails. You can organise your documents in exactly the same way that you group together applications on the iPad mini home screen by simply dragging one over another and selecting a name for the resulting folder. Add new documents to

existing folders by repeating the operation, this time dragging the new document onto the existing folder container.

The iWork applications indicate which documents need to be uploaded to the server by overlaying one corner with a

white arrow. As soon as you have adequate network coverage and it is able to complete the transfer, this arrow disappears. When there are no arrows on display you know your work has been secured remotely.

In the same manner, documents that need to be downloaded from the server are overlaid by a blue progress bar that monitors the state of the download. Once all of these bars have disappeared (they also overlay any incoming folders) you know that it's safe to kill your iPad mini's network connection as you have a complete set of your data stored locally.

Mac users running OS X 10.8 or later can also access their iCloud-stored work directly. From the template chooser, click Choose Existing Document, and then use the iCloud button at the top of the file management dialogue to flip the panel around, where you'll find a copy of the files synchronised from your iPad mini.

You won't always want to work directly off the server, so compatible OS X applications include buttons to switch between iCloud documents and those stored locally.

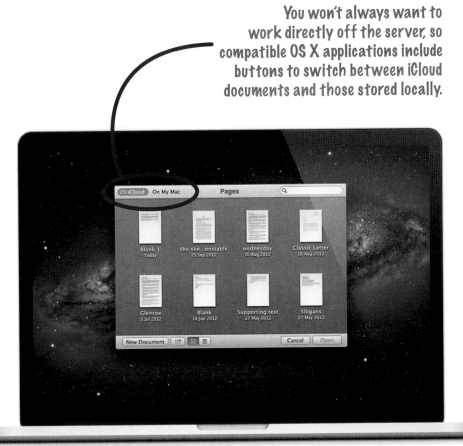

Chapter 4
Troubleshooting your iPad mini

Security

Keep your iPad mini – and your data – safe

We all carry an awful lot of information on our iPhones, iPads and iPad minis. Even if you haven't tapped it all in yourself, there's a good chance that if you're using iCloud to synchronise data with your iPad mini, it at least contains the names, addresses and phone numbers of all of your family, friends and work colleagues. It probably also contains a couple of weeks' worth of emails, and Safari may have saved the passwords that you need to use to access your online bank and other financial institutions.

Should any of this fall into the wrong hands, it could prove to be little short of a data goldmine. For this reason, it's important to make sure that your iPad mini has adequate security measures in place.

iOS 6 has three levels of security that you can enable depending upon how seriously you want to protect your data. At its most basic, you can employ a four digit code. At the opposite end of the scale, you can use a

lengthy string of characters and the threat of an automatic wipe of the iPad mini if the string is entered incorrectly too many times.

Setting a code

At the very least you should set a passcode lock on your iPad mini that needs to be entered every time it's switched on. Doing so will also enable you to set parental controls, which we'll cover in the next section.

Open the Settings application and tap General | Passcode Lock. You'll see that by default there's no lock enabled. Turn Passcode on and enter a four digit code of your choice.

Think carefully about the code that you choose. You want to

The option to set a Simple Passcode lets you choose four digits to lock your iPad mini. Avoid choosing anything too obvious.

When setting a more complex Passcode, take advantage of the extra keyboards to include less common non-alphanumeric characters.

pick one that would be easy for you to remember but not one that someone else could guess.

Avoid obvious combinations like 1234, 0000 or well-known dates such as 1066 or 1812. Also avoid using your birthday or any part of it as this information isn't particularly difficult to discover and even a mediocre identity thief would think to use it if they had it at their disposal.

You need to enter the passcode twice so that the iPad mini is sure you didn't enter it incorrectly the first time around. When you've done so, test it by turning off your iPad mini, turning back on and entering the code.

If for some reason your code isn't recognised or you forget what it is in the future, you'll need to connect the iPad mini to iTunes and reset it. If you have enabled iCloud you shouldn't lose any data in doing this, but it's important always to take a backup at regular intervals.

Setting a more complex passcode

The four digit passcode is a good first step in securing your iPad mini, as there are 10,000 possible combinations that would need to be sifted through before your thief could find their way in.

However, as we've already said, it's all too easy to pick a code that's a little bit obvious in some way, either because it's personally relevant to yourself or to the world at large.

If you are storing sensitive data on your iPad mini you should therefore consider using a more complex passcode instead.

Return to the Settings application and tap General | Passcode lock. You'll need to enter the passcode you've already set to go any further. Once you have, tap the slider

beside Simple Passcode so that it switches to OFF and enter your existing passcode again.

Your iPad mini will now ask you to enter a new passcode. You'll notice that it's swapped out the four numeral boxes for a free-form text field. Use this to type in a more complex string of characters. If possible, mix regular letters and numbers with non-alphanumeric characters, such as the ampersand, pound sign and dollar sign. You'll find these on the extended keyboards. Also mix upper and lowercase characters.

A common tactic is to replace letters with digits, such as using a zero in place of an O, a number one in place of an L or I, number four in place of an A and so on. Doing this and throwing in a handful of non-regular characters increases the strength of your more complex passcode.

Automatic wipe

Your last line of defence, and the most drastic option, is to set your iPad mini to wipe itself clean

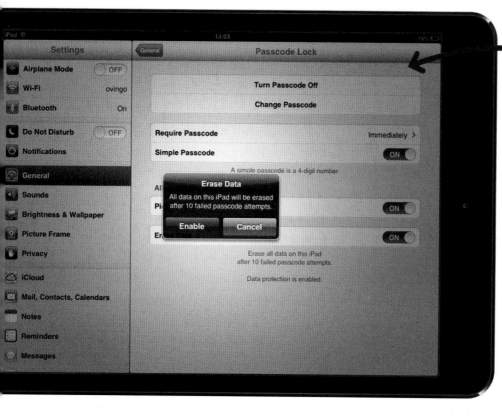

Setting your iPad mini to wipe itself if someone enters the Passcode incorrectly 10 times in a row is a highly effective way to keep your data secure.

of all data should anyone enter an incorrect passcode 10 times in a row. Obviously, this is fairly drastic, but it would stop anyone accessing your files if they didn't have the correct login details.

It's enabled by tapping the Erase Data slider. It has implications for the retention of your information, so iOS ensures you really do want to enable it by throwing up a dialogue asking for your confirmation.

Security vs convenience

If you frequently turn your iPad mini on and off, or you sometimes allow it to go to sleep on its own, it can be annoying having to enter the passcode again as soon as you want to turn it back on. In an instance such as this, you want to increase the length of time that your iPad mini needs to have been turned off for before asking you to enter the passcode again.

There's a fairly good chance that should anyone steal your iPad mini they won't turn it on immediately. They'll be more interested in getting as far away from you as they can with the greatest discretion so that you don't spot that they have your

property tucked under their arm. Likewise, should you leave your iPad mini on the back seat of a taxi or on the luggage rack of a train, it will probably be a little while before somebody picks it up and turns it on.

This means that the only likely scenario in which somebody would immediately turn on and use your iPad mini without your permission would be if it was in your home or your workplace. So, you might want to extend the period of time that the iPad mini can sleep for before asking for the passcode as people in those environments are likely to be more trustworthy.

To do this, return to the Passcode Lock screens and tap Require Passcode, then choose whether it should be required immediately or after a specified delay, depending on the balance

If you find yourself entering the Passcode more often than you'd like, consider lengthening the intervals that your iPad mini can sleep for before it's required.

you want to strike between data security and the convenience of being able to pick up your iPad mini, switch it on and get working right away without being interrupted by a demand to once again enter your passcode.

Ultimately, implementing an effective security policy is always a matter of striking a careful balance of acceptable convenience for yourself and maximum inconvenience for any possible malcontent. Your job is to work out where that balance lies and set the iPad mini's built-in checks and controls to accommodate.

Quick Tip: Auto-Lock

The Auto-Lock isn't a security feature, but it's worth considering at the same time as choosing an appropriate time out for the Passcode Lock.

Auto-Lock is the function that dims your iPad mini's screen after a set period of inactivity and then, a few seconds later, turns it off entirely.

If you're performing a task that doesn't require you to tap the screen frequently, such as reading a long tract of text, you may find that your iPad mini dims and turns off before you've got to the end of your task. This would require you to turn it back on and, if your Passcode is set to be applied immediately, you'd have to enter the code before you could finish what you are doing. This interrupts your workflow.

You can avoid this problem by setting the Auto-Lock to only kick in after a longer period of inactivity. Open the Settings application and tap General | Auto-Lock, then select how long your iPad mini should wait before going to sleep.

If you want to disable Auto-Lock entirely, pick 'Never'. If 'Never' doesn't appear on the list of options on your iPad mini, then it may have been disabled by one of your configured email accounts. Various online forums report some users discovering that particular Exchange Server configurations make this option inaccessible. In that case, unless you want to disable your email account, take the next best option which is to set Auto-Lock to kick in after the longest possible delay.

Find My iPad

How to trace a lost or stolen iPad mini

Apple recognises that as many of us will take our iPad minis everywhere we go there's always a chance we could lose them. This might be a result of a completely innocent mix-up, as we could leave them on the bus or in a cafe, or it could be more malicious with our gadgets stolen from our bags.

However you still want the best chance possible of finding your iPad mini again or, if it's been taken dishonestly, at least removing all of your data to keep it safe from prying eyes.

We've already covered implementing the Passcode wipe, but for complete peace of mind you also want to use Find My iPhone. Originally developed to calm business users' worries, it's a boon for consumers and, despite the name, it works just as well with the iPad and iPad mini.

What is Find My iPhone

Find My iPhone (also called Find My iPad) is a smart service that uses iCloud to locate your iPad mini anywhere in the world using its GPS chip (if it has cellphone network connectivity) or an active Wi-Fi connection.

It relies on you having at least one iCloud email account active on the device, which is set to receive push email. If you don't have this set up, tap Settings | Mail, Contacts, Calendars | Add Account... and select iCloud from the list of account type options.

Activate Find My iPad

Find My iPad is turned off by default. This makes sense as it relies on passing your current location through the iCloud servers, which some users may consider to be a security risk. To turn it on, tap Settings | iCloud and tap the ON/OFF slider beside Find My iPad.

Log in to your account at *icloud.com* using a regular browser and select Find My

Find my iPhone application

If you have several iOS devices, you can use each one to find any of the others that you have lost. Apple has produced a Find my iPhone app, which can search for iPads, iPad minis, iPhones, iPod touches and Apple's desktop and laptop computers. Search the App Store for *Find My iPhone* to download it for free.

iPhone. If you don't see this option on the front page, you'll be in one of the other modules already, so click the cloud icon in he upper corner to return to the iCloud home screen.

Right away iCloud starts searching for each of the devices that you've registered to your account and plotting them on a map. You can switch between them by clicking the Devices button above the map and selecting them from the list. You can also switch between a zoomable map, satellite and hybrid views to help you zoom in to the closest possible location.

Select the device that you need to locate – in our case an iPad mini – and it will be highlighted on the map using a pushpin. At the same time, a floating panel appears in the upper right corner with options for remotely controlling your iPad mini: playing a sound, remotely

locking it with Lost Mode, and wiping it completely (see left).

Your first step should always be to play a message so that you can see whether you've simply misplaced it close at hand.

If you can't hear it beeping then you should move on to the next steps: lost mode or wipe.

In lost mode, the iPad can only be unlocked using a security code you specify. The iPad mini will be set to display a blank

screen with a dialogue in the middle showing a phone number and message (see below). When the person who has it swipes to unlock, they're asked to enter the code. If they can't, they won't be able to use your iPad mini. If you have also set it to wipe itself after 10 incorrect attempts, they have limited opportunities.

Your last line of defence is the remote wipe carried out directly through *icloud.com*. You should only do this if you're sure that you're not going to get your iPad back as it's impossible to locate it again using Find My iPhone once it's been wiped.

Location Services
How to control which apps know where you are

Find My iPad relies on the iPad mini's built in Location Services tools to pass data about your location back to Apple's servers.

Because these tools know a lot about your movements and could be used to track you, it's worth considering them in the scope of your general security and privacy, even though Apple is unlikely to ever do anything underhand with the data gathered.

Location Services benefits

The accuracy with which your iPad mini can get a fix on your current location depends upon the model you own, with the non-cellular iPad mini relying solely on a reverse look-up of your address on a wireless network and its built-in compass. The cellular-enabled iPad mini adds to this the ability to triangulate its position on the cellphone network and a built-in GPS and GLONASS receiver, which interprets data received from orbiting satellites.

Besides stamping your photos, this data is used for a wide range of purposes by a whole host of third-party applications so that they can offer you vouchers and discounts on the basis of your location, walk you step by step through a series of directions on a map, or tag your posts to social networks with your location at the time of writing.

Like the iPhone, iPod touch and full-size iPad, it can also use Location Services to geo-stamp any photos you take, so long as you enable your third-party camera app to use this data.

Tagging photos with accurate longitude and latitude geocodes means they can be plotted on a map, both inside the phone itself and when offloaded to external software such as Adobe Lightroom and Apple iPhoto, or to a photo sharing site like Flickr.

This feature isn't turned on by default, so to enable Location Services tap Settings | Privacy | Location Services and check that the slider at the top of the screen is set to on (see below).

This slider lets you quickly enable or disable all of your location services, with individual controls for each application that

Tap a pushpin to display a stack of thumbnails for the photos taken in that location. Tapping the stack opens the constituent images in their own album view.

has requested access to your location over time listed below.

You'll notice that in the grab to the left there's a small grey arrow beside Find My iPad. That indicates that the app has used our location in the last 24 hours. If the arrow was purple it would mean that the application was using our location right

now, and if it was a hollow purple arrow it would be using what's known as a geofence to monitor our position within a specified area.

You can view any photos in your Camera Roll that have been geo-stamped directly on your iPad mini. Open the Photos application and tap

the Places button on the top toolbar. You'll see that all the spots where you've taken photos are marked using a red pushpin.

Unpinch on the screen to separate them, then tap on a pin to reveal how many photos were taken there. Tapping the bubble that pops up reveals thumbnails of just those images (above).

Parental controls
Keeping younger users safe

Apple has been slightly inconsistent when it comes to tailoring the specific abilities and content of an iPad, iPad mini, iPhone and iPod touch, when compared with a Mac or PC.

If you want to keep your children away from content you feel is inappropriate for them, you should turn to Parental Controls in iTunes' Preferences on your Mac or PC, and to Restrictions on the iPad (tap Settings | General | Restrictions).

Both of these let you exert increasing levels of control over what can be downloaded and installed until you get to the point where you're happy allowing younger users to get their hands on your iPad mini unsupervised.

Parental Controls apply in both iTunes on the Mac and PC, and on the iPad mini itself, where they're activated in the Settings app.

Locking down your iPad mini

To invoke restrictions on your iPad mini, open Settings and tap General | Restrictions | Enable Restrictions and choose a four-digit security code (see opposite

page). This must be entered when making any changes to your settings, and so should stop your children disabling them once you've set them in place.

With restrictions enabled you can disable whole applications, such as Safari, YouTube and iTunes, forbid App Store installations and switch off the Location Services described on the previous page.

Of greatest interest is the media ratings system, which can

On the iPad mini, parental controls are handled using the in-built Restrictions function, which has been localised with regionally-relevant film and TV ratings for territories right around the world.

be tailored for specific regional and national territories. The range of options open to you here has expended massively with the release of iOS 6.

Choosing your home territory will let you pick from restrictions that match the ratings you'll already know from the cinema and DVDs. So, pick UK and you'll have movie ratings of U, Uc, PG, 12, 12A, 15 and 18. Switch to Ireland, though, and you'll be able to choose from G, PG, 12, 15, 16 and 18.

These national variations don't just apply to downloaded movies, though. In the UK you have a fairly narrow set of options when it comes to television shows, as you can allow all or no TV shows, or just those rated for 'Caution'. In the US, though, where regulations are different, you have 16 ratings from TV-Y to TV-MA.

In all countries, the choices for podcasts are simply on or off for explicit content, but the options for applications are more extensive and match Apple's own App Store ratings system.

In practice, the best policy is usually to employ restrictions of this type in concert with supervised use, to help educate children and explain anything that might still slip through.

Notifications

Controlling when, where and how they appear

Apple considerably simplified the way that its mobile devices handle notifications with the arrival of iOS 6 when it introduced Notification Centre.

Notification Centre, as its name suggests, groups together all of the alerts that sound on your iPad mini, from any installed application, and makes them easy to find in a single pull-down panel. To view it, put your finger on the clock at the top of the screen and drag down.

Notification Centre is controlled through the Notifications section of the centralised iOS Settings app.

Notifications

In earlier versions of iOS there was only one alert type: a bezel that appeared at the centre of the screen. In iOS 6 you can select from three alert styles: the old-style alert, a banner that briefly rolls down from the top of the screen, and no alert at all.

Even if you select the option not to use live alerts, your applications will still post their alerts to Notification Centre if they are in the Notification Centre group so that they're easy to find when you need to give them some attention.

To select a notification type, open Settings | Notifications and then select the application that you want to tweak from the two lists, one of which handles items that appear in Notification Centre and those that don't. It's up to you which list includes each app.

Tap the application you want to configure and work your way through the interface that appears, allowing you to decide whether or not it should appear in Notification Centre, how many alerts should be archived in the Centre, what kind of Alert it should use and so on.

The option to display a Badge App Icon turns on and off the red numbers that appear on the corners of some application icons to show how many unattended

Dragging down from the clock at the top of the screen opens Notification Centre, which gathers together each of your alerts.

Notifications settings screens

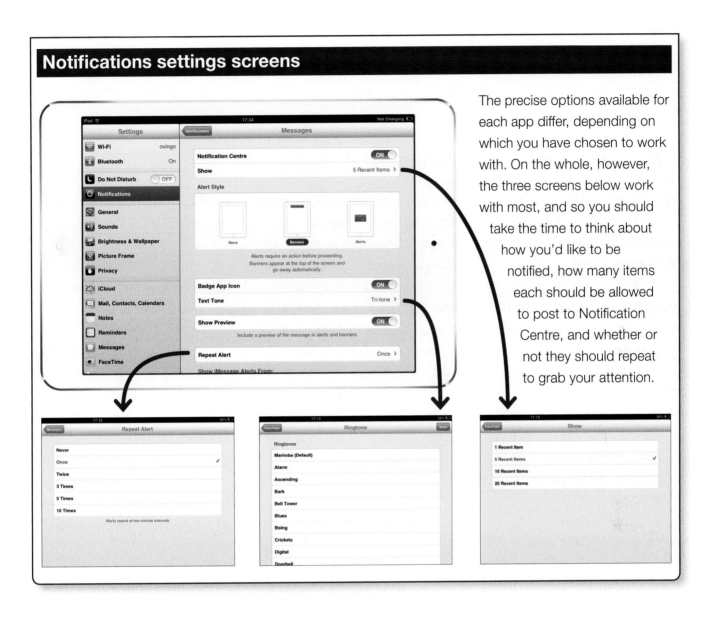

The precise options available for each app differ, depending on which you have chosen to work with. On the whole, however, the three screens below work with most, and so you should take the time to think about how you'd like to be notified, how many items each should be allowed to post to Notification Centre, and whether or not they should repeat to grab your attention.

notifications they are waiting for you to deal with.

Not all of the applications configured here have the same range of options, but they each have a general structure, which means that when you are familiar with one you shouldn't have any trouble configuring the others. Just don't forget to examine the

supplementary panes for each one, as shown in the boxed-out grabs above, to access their complete range of available settings.

With our notifications set up and working the way we want, we can move on to consider when they should and shouldn't be allowed to intrude.

Avoiding distractions

It's always been possible – since the arrival of the very first iPhone – to flip a switch on the side of the handset to mute the speaker on an iOS device when you don't want it to sound. This is particularly useful when you're riding in a quiet coach on the

At its most basic, Do Not Disturb is a simple on or off option, but by digging a little deeper you can customise it.

Automatic suppression

Tap Notifications | Do Not Disturb to open its options if you want to take things further. Here, you can schedule the Do Not Disturb feature to kick in automatically during certain hours of the day so that you don't need to remember to switch it on manually each time you need some peace and quiet.

This scheduling facility would be useful for anyone who works shifts and wouldn't want to be disturbed during the day if they were sleeping. However, it can be just as useful for anyone who shouldn't be disturbed while at work, such as a teacher standing at the front of a classroom who

If you get disturbed by your iPad mini when you should be sleeping, you can specify times when it shouldn't sound alerts.

train, or visiting a location, such as a church or museum, when an iPad mini pinging to inform you about new incoming emails would attract some frowns. However, with iOS 6 you can go much further, courtesy of a fully-fledged Do Not Disturb feature. You'll find it through Settings | Do

Not Disturb and simply tap the slider to activate it.

This prevents apps sounding alerts when they reach your iPad mini, however important they are, so that while you'll still be able to send emails, messages, tweets and so on yourself, and it will receive incoming messages, it will act as though it's switched off in the incoming direction. It also silences any application alerts that might fire, such as Twitter or Reminders.

Two quick tips for silencing your iPad mini

You can quickly silence your iPad mini by holding the hardware volume down button, which mutes it completely, or swipe up with four fingers anywhere on the screen to call up the task switching bar, swipe this to the right and use the volume control that you'll have just uncovered to drag the volume down to zero.

naturally won't want to have an iPad mini in their bag chiming in the presence of students who have been told that this kind of behaviour is a sign of disrespect.

You'll notice that when it's active the feature puts a moon icon beside the clock, regardless of the time of day, to indicate that it's active.

iOS 6 recognises that there are times when it's important certain people can still get through to

Below: You can be selective about who is able to reach you when alerts are suppressed by creating white lists.

you, even if your iPad mini is set to this mode. For example, you may be a parent whose children have locked themselves out of the house, or be caring for a sick relative who needs to call on FaceTime you at short notice.

In these instances you would set the iPad mini to allow through calls from a particular group in your Contacts list. By default it is anyone who has been set as a Favourite, but you can alternatively change this to any defined group. So, you could

trim down the list yet further by organising just close family members into a new list and setting that as the only group of people who can break the Do Not Disturb rule.

If even this would be too much, tap Settings | Notifications | Do Not Disturb | Allow Calls From and select No One.

The final option is to decide how your iPad mini should handle repeated FaceTime calls.

iOS 6 considers any call that comes in from the same person within three minutes or less to be a repeated call, and it's set to let these through regardless of whether or not your iPad mini is set to Do Not Disturb (even if you've set the Allow Calls option to 'No One').

The logic here is that anyone who urgently needs to speak to you is more likely to call you again right away rather than leave a message. Again, you can disable this by tapping the ON/OFF slider beside Repeated Calls.

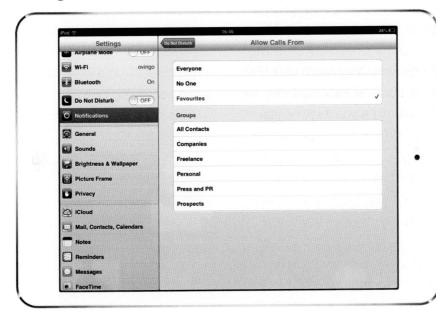

Streaming

Enjoy your media on the big screen and better speakers

AirPlay is an extremely easy to use software technology that makes it easy to direct audio and video around your home network.

Compatible devices supporting Apple's AirPlay protocols, such as Apple TV, AirPort Express and third-party speakers and Docks, advertise their presence on the network so that they can be detected by the iPhone, iPad mini, iPad, iPod touch or Macs running iTunes (or any other regular desktop or laptop application running inside OS X 10.8 Mountain Lion).

Once an AirPlay device is connected to your network and plugged in, you only need to fire up one of the iOS audio or video apps to put it to use.

Here we're using Music, the app that replaced iPod in iOS 5

The AirPlay icon, circled below, lets you choose where to direct the output of an iPad mini media-playback app.

and 6 to stream an album over our home network from the iPad mini to a set of speakers in a room downstairs.

The speakers are connected to an AirPort Express, and we know that the iPad mini has spotted it because Music displays the AirPlay icon beside the volume control (see the circled icon, below left). Tapping this lets us select the output destination from the range of detected devices on the network (see grab, below).

The full range of Music controls is still available through the iPad mini even though it's not the output device receiving the stream, so we don't need to get up and walk over to the connected speaker to change the volume or skip forwards or backwards through the available tracks on our album.

Dragging the slider on the iPad's Music app changes the volume being fed to the speaker, and the regular transport controls (forwards, backwards and so on)

It's long been rumoured that Apple is plotting its entry into the home TV market. Until it does (if indeed that's the plan) you'll have to make use of its diminutive Apple TV add-on box instead

still work on the iPhone the same way they would if you were using headphones.

AirPlay doesn't only handle music and streamed audio, though. Apple has also built the technology into its video applications and produces a dedicated set-top box called Apple TV through which you can stream 1080p high definition video straight through to an HD

television as though the iPad mini was directly connected.

Apple TV is built to work with media downloaded from the iTunes Store, so it's perfect for streaming movies, either directly or from your iPad mini, and can also be used to share YouTube and other online video sites with

your friends without everyone squeezing around your screen.

In a business context, Apple TV and AirPlay make it easy to give presentations from the iPad mini because it can wirelessly stream slides, such as those created using Keynote, direct to the screen, thus obviating the need to buy a video connection kit to hook it up to a projector or other third-party kit.

Glossary
Common terms and technology explained

802.11A/b/g/n Wireless communications standards. See Wi-Fi.

Bitrate Means of expressing the number of audio samples processed in a set period of time, usually a second. See also kilobits per second.

Bluetooth Short-range radio networking standard, allowing compatible devices to 'see' and interrogate each other to discover their shared abilities and then use these abilities to swap information. It is commonly used to connect tablets like the iPad mini to keyboard, but can also be used to share data such as images from iPhoto, or contacts from the address book.

Compression When images on a website or music on an iPad mini or iPhone are made smaller so that they either download more quickly or take up less space in the device's memory they are said to have been compressed. Compression involves selectively removing

parts of the file that are less easily seen or heard by the human eye and ear and simplifying the more complex parts.

Digital Rights Management DRM. Additional encoded data added to a digitised piece of audio or video that controls the way in which it will work, usually preventing it from being shared among several users. See also FairPlay.

Encoding The process of capturing an analogue data source, such as a sound or an image, and translating it into a digital format. Although files can be encoded with no loss of quality, the process usually also involves compression to reduce the resulting file sizes.

FairPlay Digital rights management system developed and used by Apple. It is a closed, proprietary system that Apple has so far refused to license to third-party software and hardware manufacturers, or to

music owners on the basis that this could lead to its compromise.

Firewall Hardware or software device the controls the flow of data in and out of a machine or network. It can also help to rebuff attacks from hackers. Frequently used by network administrators to ensure that local users do not access external services that could compromise the integrity of the network.

GB Gigabyte. One billion bytes, and a means of measuring the capacity of a device. A byte is made up of eight bits, and a bit is equivalent to a single character, such as a, b, c, 4, 5, 6 and so on. As digital files are encoded

using the characters 0 and 1, each digit that makes up part of its encoding will represent one bit, every eight characters will make one byte, every 1,024 bytes will equal a kilobyte and every billion bytes will equate to a gigabyte. To put this into context, the iPad mini has a capacity of up to 64GB. If this was devoted entirely to music, then by multiplying up Apple's calculations for the 32GB iPod touch, it would be able to hold about 14,000 songs at iTunes' default settings, although in practice few iPad minis will ever carry this much music as some space will have to be given over to contacts, photos and so on.

Home Screen As used within this book, the term used to describe the screen within the iPad mini's interface that displays the icons for the installed applications (see above right).

iCloud Online synchronisation service run from several data centres around the world. Provides backup for iPhones,

iPads, iPad minis, iPod touches and other Apple hardware, and shares both documents and images with Macs and PCs

IMAP Internet Message Access Protocol. A server-based means of hosting incoming and outgoing email messages such that they can be accessed using a remote client such as the iPad mini, iPad or iPhone. The primary benefit of working in this way is that the messages will always be accessible from any device, anywhere and at any time.

iOS Short for iPhone Operating System. The underlying software that enables your iPad mini to start up and run third-party applications. Currently on its sixth revision – iOS 6 – it is based on the same code as OS X and was previously called iPhone OS, despite its use on the iPod touch.

iPod Portable music player made by Apple. First introduced in October 2001, and since expanded to encompass, over time, the mini, nano (see opposite

page), classic and touch and shuffle versions.

iTunes Music management software produced by Apple, also used to manage the connection between an iPad mini and Mac or PC. It gives access to the iTunes Store for purchasing music, audiobooks and video content, and will also handle podcast subscriptions.

Kilobits per second (Kbps) A measurement of the number of audio samples that go to make each second of music in a digitally encoded track such as those played by Music app. The higher this number, the smoother the sound wave will be, and the truer to the original it will sound.

127

MAC address Machine Access Code address. A unique hexadecimal number organised into six pairs of digits that identifies the wireless hardware inside a device such as a computer or the iPad mini. As no two devices can ever have the same MAC address, this string of numbers is often used as an identifier to restrict access to wireless access points and other Wi-Fi- or Bluetooth-enabled devices.

Megapixel One million pixels. A measurement used to quantify the ability of a digital camera to capture information. The higher the megapixel measurement, the more information it will capture, leading to larger file sizes, but allowing for the captured image to be either printed on a larger scale or cropped to highlight smaller details. It is a common misconception that higher megapixel counts lead to sharper images, which is not always the case, as image crispness often depends as much on the quality of the lens in front of the sensor and the relative size, rather than resolution, of the sensor itself.

MP3 Shorthand term used to denote audio tracks encoded using the Motion Picture Expert Group codec 2 (Mpeg-2), level three. Arguably the most common audio format found on the web thanks to its widespread use by portable music players. Capable of being read by the iPad mini and iPod, but it is not Apple's preferred format.

OS X Operating system developed by Apple, a variant of which is used inside the iPad mini and later versions of the iPod under the name iOS. It shares a common core with Apple's modern operating system for laptop and desktop computers, Mac OS X, which was developed from code it inherited when it acquired Steve Jobs' NeXT computer company. The X in its name is pronounced 'ten' since it is the tenth major iteration of the operating system.

Playlist Menu of audio tracks or video files waiting to be played. The iPhone, iPad, iPad mini and iPod are all able to share playlists with those created on a computer using iTunes.

Podcast Pre-recorded audio or video programme distributed over the Internet and optimised for playback on portable devices such as the iPod and iPad mini.

Pop3 Post Office Protocol 3. This is the predominant technology for email delivery used by most consumer-level Internet service providers. All good email clients, including the version of Mail that is built into the iPad mini, can use this protocol to receive email.

The rear camera on the iPad mini has a 5 megapixel resolution; the one at the front has 1.2 megapixels.

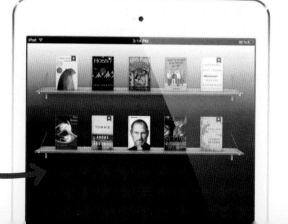

128

Push email The technology by which emails are sent from the central server that holds them to a client device, such as a mobile phone or BlackBerry, without the owner having to manually instigate a retrieval for their messages. This is implemented on the iPad mini through Apple's own iCloud service (see above).

Rip A term used to describe the act of extracting audio from a CD for digital playback on a device such as the iPad mini.

SIM Subscriber Identity Module. The small half-stamp-sized (or smaller) card found in cellular-enabled devices that identifies them on the network, containing their number and other data.

SMS Short Message Service. Commonly referred to as text messages, SMS is a means of sending brief notes between mobile handsets, which was initially developed as a means for network operators to send messages to their subscribers. SMS messages are generally restricted to 160 characters or fewer, although Apple's own Messages application, which is found on the iPad mini and iPhone allows for longer messages, and even file transfers.

SMTP Simple Mail Transfer Protocol. This is the most common – almost default – means of sending email from any client that works on the basis of

composing messages using a standalone client rather than a web-based system such as Imap, as used by the iCloud service, or the Exchange system developed by Microsoft and popular in businesses, both of which make it possible to store outgoing messages on the server so that they can be synchronised across multiple devices.

SSL Secure Sockets Layer. A method used to encrypt data sent across wireless connections and the Internet so that it is less easy for uninvited third parties to intercept and decode.

Sync Short for synchronise. The means of swapping data between the iPad mini and a desktop or laptop computer so that the information on each – including music, photos, contacts and so on – mirrors the other. Traditionally performed by connecting the two using the bundled Lightning connector cable, although Apple now enables wireless synchronisation on a local Wi-Fi network for those

devices running at least iOS 5 or later connecting to iTunes 10.5.

Toolbar Any area within a piece of software that houses buttons to perform common functions.

USB Universal Serial Bus. A socket, plug and cable system that allows almost any peripheral to be connected to a Mac or PC, including printers, mice, keyboards and so on. The iPad mini, iPad, iPhone and iPod also use USB as a means of exchanging data with a computer and, as the cable can carry power, charging their batteries. The iPad mini uses Apple's new Lightning connector, although some older devices use a larger 30-pin dock connector.

VBR Variable Bit Rate. A means of varying the effective audio resolution of a sound file, such as a song, based on the complexity of its contents. More complex sections of a track will thus have a higher bitrate, while less complex parts will be more heavily compressed.

Wi-Fi or **Wifi** Once colloquial, but now a generally accepted term for wireless networking. It embodies several standards, of which the four most common are 802.11a, 802.11b, 802.11g and 802.11n. The 'a' and 'g' variants can each achieve a maximum data throughput of 54 megabits per second, while 802.11b runs at 11 megabits per second. 802.11n, the fastest standard

at 248 megabits per second, is as yet unratified, although draft standards have allowed it to be built into many wireless devices already, giving it good overall industry support. The iPad mini uses 802.11b, g and n for the widest possible compatibility.

Wireless Access Point Hardware device that connects to your network or broadband connection and replicates the features of wired networks in a wireless form to provide network and Internet access to Wi-Fi devices such as the iPhone, iPad or iPod touch.

WMA Acronym for Windows Media Audio. A file format developed by Microsoft, enjoying good industry support, although conspicuous in its absence from the iPhone, iPad, iPad mini and iPod. It is the preferred format for many non-Apple online music stores due to its ability to include strong anti-piracy measures inside the encoded file.